Top Year 5 Times Tables Tests from CGP!

Times Tables are a really important part of Maths, that's for sure —
the only way to master them is regular practice throughout the year.

That's where this CGP book comes in. It's packed with pupil-friendly
10-Minute Workouts — one for every week of Year 5. Each one covers
a mixture of Times Tables skills to keep them on their toes.

We've included all the answers in a cut-out section, and there's even
a progress chart to help keep track of pupils' scores. Smashing!

Published by CGP
ISBN: 978 1 78908 365 1

Editors: Rachael Rogers, Sarah Pattison and Caroline Purvis

With thanks to Nicola Paddock, Glenn Rogers and
Karen Wells for the proofreading.

With thanks to Jan Greenway for the copyright research.

Clipart from Corel®

Contains public sector information licensed under
the Open Government Licence v3.0 http://www.
nationalarchives.gov.uk/doc/open-government-licence/
version/3/

Printed by Elanders Ltd, Newcastle upon Tyne.

Based on the classic CGP style created by Richard Parsons.

Text, design, layout and original illustrations
© Coordination Group Publications Ltd. (CGP) 2019
All rights reserved.

Photocopying this book is not permitted, even if you have a CLA licence.
Extra copies are available from CGP with next day delivery • 0800 1712 712 • www.cgpbooks.co.uk

How to Use this Book

- This book contains 36 workouts. We've split them into 3 sections — one for each term, with 12 workouts each. There's roughly one workout for every week of the school year.

- Each workout is out of 20 marks and should take about 10 minutes.

- Each workout starts with some quick fire questions, before moving on to some trickier questions such as worded problems. Pupils are encouraged to time how long it takes them to do each workout.

- Each workout ends with a fun puzzle to challenge pupils who finish the timed section. Some puzzles draw on other maths skills that pupils will have already covered.

- The workouts increase in difficulty as you go through the book.

- Problems requiring knowledge of Year 5 level maths skills are not introduced until the Summer Term.

- Answers and a Progress Chart can be found at the back of the book.

The contents pages show where each times table is tested, and any extra maths tested in the puzzles.

The workouts in each term can be done in any order — you can pick the workout which best suits the needs of your class.

The tick boxes on the contents pages can help you to keep a record of which workouts have been attempted.

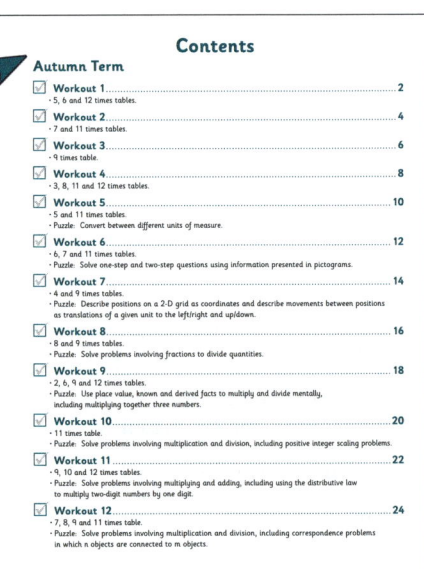

Contents

Autumn Term

☑ **Workout 1** 2
  • 5, 6 and 12 times tables.

☑ **Workout 2** 4
  • 7 and 11 times tables.

☑ **Workout 3** 6
  • 9 times table.

☑ **Workout 4** 8
  • 3, 8, 11 and 12 times tables.

☑ **Workout 5** 10
  • 5 and 11 times tables.
  • Puzzle: Convert between different units of measure.

☑ **Workout 6** 12
  • 6, 7 and 11 times tables.
  • Puzzle: Solve one-step and two-step questions using information presented in pictograms.

☑ **Workout 7** 14
  • 4 and 9 times tables.
  • Puzzle: Describe positions on a 2-D grid as coordinates and describe movements between positions as translations of a given unit to the left/right and up/down.

☑ **Workout 8** 16
  • 8 and 9 times tables.
  • Puzzle: Solve problems involving fractions to divide quantities.

☑ **Workout 9** 18
  • 2, 6, 9 and 12 times tables.
  • Puzzle: Use place value, known and derived facts to multiply and divide mentally, including multiplying together three numbers.

☑ **Workout 10** 20
  • 11 times table.
  • Puzzle: Solve problems involving multiplication and division, including positive integer scaling problems.

☑ **Workout 11** 22
  • 9, 10 and 12 times tables.
  • Puzzle: Solve problems involving multiplying and adding, including using the distributive law to multiply two-digit numbers by one digit.

☑ **Workout 12** 24
  • 7, 8, 9 and 11 times table.
  • Puzzle: Solve problems involving multiplication and division, including correspondence problems in which n objects are connected to m objects.

Spring Term

- [✓] **Workout 1** 26
  - 6 and 7 times tables.
- [✓] **Workout 2** 28
  - 7, 9, 10 and 12 times tables.
- [✓] **Workout 3** 30
  - 9 and 11 times tables.
- [✓] **Workout 4** 32
  - 5, 7, 10 and 12 times tables.
  - Puzzle: Read Roman numerals to 100 (I to C).
- [✓] **Workout 5** 34
  - 2, 7 and 12 times tables.
  - Puzzle: Use place value, known and derived facts to multiply and divide mentally.
- [✓] **Workout 6** 36
  - 5, 6, 11 and 12 times tables.
  - Puzzle: Estimate, compare and calculate different measures, including money in pounds and pence.
- [✓] **Workout 7** 38
  - 12 times table.
  - Puzzle: Recognise and show, using diagrams, families of common equivalent fractions.
- [✓] **Workout 8** 40
  - 3 and 7 times tables.
  - Puzzle: Solve comparison, sum and difference problems using information presented in bar charts.
- [✓] **Workout 9** 42
  - 3, 4 and 11 times tables.
  - Puzzle: Solve problems, including correspondence problems in which n objects are connected to m objects.
- [✓] **Workout 10** 44
  - 5, 8, 9 and 11 times tables.
  - Puzzle: Solve problems involving multiplying and adding, including using the distributive law to multiply two-digit numbers by one digit.
- [✓] **Workout 11** 46
  - 6 and 9 times tables.
  - Puzzle: Solve problems, including integer scaling problems.
- [✓] **Workout 12** 48
  - 2, 9 and 11 times tables.
  - Puzzle: Solve two-step problems in contexts, choosing the appropriate operation.

Summer Term

☑ **Workout 1** **50**
  • 8 and 12 times tables.

☑ **Workout 2** **52**
  • 4, 6, 7 and 11 times tables.

☑ **Workout 3** **54**
  • 3, 7 and 10 times tables.
  • Puzzle: Solve problems involving multiplication and division, including scaling by simple fractions.

☑ **Workout 4** **56**
  • 3, 4 and 12 times tables.
  • Puzzle: Calculate and compare the area of rectangles.

☑ **Workout 5** **58**
  • 6, 7, 8 and 11 times tables.
  • Puzzle: Establish whether a number up to 100 is prime and recall prime numbers up to 19.

☑ **Workout 6** **60**
  • 7 times table.
  • Puzzle: Use approximate equivalences between metric units and common imperial units such as inches, pounds and pints.

☑ **Workout 7** **62**
  • 4, 7, 9 and 11 times tables.
  • Puzzle: Divide numbers up to 4 digits by a one-digit number and interpret remainders appropriately.

☑ **Workout 8** **64**
  • Mixed times tables.
  • Puzzle: Identify multiples and factors, including finding all factor pairs of a number.

☑ **Workout 9** **66**
  • 6 times table.
  • Puzzle: Recognise mixed numbers and improper fractions and convert from one form to the other.

☑ **Workout 10** **68**
  • 7, 8 and 10 times tables.

☑ **Workout 11** **70**
  • Mixed times tables.
  • Puzzle: Complete, read and interpret information in tables, including timetables.

☑ **Workout 12** **72**
  • Mixed times tables.
  • Puzzle: Compare and order fractions whose denominators are all multiples of the same number.

Times Tables Chart **74**

Answers **75**

Autumn Term: Workout 1

Quick fire

1. a) 5 × 5 = ...   c) 4 × 6 = ...

   b) 12 × 3 = ...   d) 5 × 12 = ...

   4 marks

2. a) 45 ÷ 5 = ...   c) 6 ÷ 1 = ...

   b) 48 ÷ 6 = ...   d) 72 ÷ 6 = ...

   4 marks

3. a) .... × 6 = 18   c) .... ÷ 6 = 9

   b) 5 × .... = 35   d) 132 ÷ .... = 11

   4 marks

4. a) What are six sixes? ....   b) How many fives make up forty? ....

   2 marks

Now try these:

5. Florence brushes her dog 4 times a week. Each brushing session lasts for 5 minutes. How many minutes does Florence spend brushing her dog each week?

   .... *1 mark*

6. Zain buys 10 packs of stickers. Each pack contains 12 stickers. How many stickers will he get?

   .... *1 mark*

7. Amelia is making friendship bracelets for 6 of her friends.
She puts 3 red beads and 4 blue beads on each bracelet.
How many coloured beads will she need altogether?

....

2 marks

8. Hanna has 6 goats and 4 donkeys on her farm.
She gives each animal 5 pieces of carrot.
How many pieces of carrot does she use?

....

2 marks

How did you do?   Time: Score:

Puzzle: Time for Doughnuts

Steve, Herbert and Helen all make doughnuts to sell.
Steve puts 5 doughnuts in each bag, Herbert puts 6 doughnuts in each bag, and Helen puts 12 doughnuts in each bag.
Tick the person below that gets the most doughnuts.

I'd like 10 bags from you Herbert and 2 bags from you Steve.

8 bags please Helen!

Herbert, 12 bags please.

Helen, I'll have 2 bags from you please. Steve, I'll have 10 bags from you please.

Puzzle Complete? ✓

Autumn Term: Workout 2

Quick fire

1. a) 3 × 7 = ...   c) 7 × 7 = ...

    b) 11 × 9 = ...   d) 11 × 10 = ...

    4 marks

2. a) 22 ÷ 11 = ...   c) 121 ÷ 11 = ...

    b) 42 ÷ 7 = ...   d) 77 ÷ 7 = ...

    4 marks

3. a) 11 × .... = 44   c) .... × 7 = 14

    b) 63 ÷ .... = 9   d) 11 ÷ .... = 1

    4 marks

4. a) What is fifty-six divided by seven? ....   b) What is eight lots of eleven? ....

    2 marks

Now try these:

5. Vasha is putting tulips in bunches of 5. She makes 7 bunches. How many tulips does she use?

    ....

    1 mark

6. Muhammed finds out 3 facts about each of the 11 players of his favourite football team. How many facts does he find out?

    ....

    1 mark

7. Maisie has 100 sequins. She puts 7 sequins on each of the 4 spaceships she's drawn. How many sequins will she have left?

    ....

    2 marks

8. Mrs Ellis has chosen 5 children from Year 4 and 7 children from Year 5 to help her decorate a Christmas tree.
She gives each child 7 decorations.
How many decorations does she give out?

.... ____
                            2 marks

How did you do?   Time: [ ]   Score: [ ]

Puzzle: Video Game Time

The number of minutes that four different children spend playing video games one Monday is shown below.

Saanvi — 7 × 10
Kia — 55 ÷ 5
Marco — 132 ÷ 11
Roddy — 11 × 6

Who spends the least amount of time playing video games?

....

How much more time does Saanvi spend playing video games than Roddy?

....

Marco spends 7 times as long playing video games on Saturday than he does on Monday. How long does Marco play video games for on Saturday?

....   **Puzzle Complete?**

Autumn Term: Workout 3

Quick fire

1. a) 2 × 9 = ...
    b) 9 × 9 = ...
    c) 7 × 9 = ...
    d) 12 × 9 = ...

    4 marks

2. a) 54 ÷ 9 = ...
    b) 63 ÷ 9 = ...
    c) 99 ÷ 11 = ...
    d) 45 ÷ 9 = ...

    4 marks

3. a) .... ÷ 9 = 8
    b) 9 ÷ .... = 9
    c) 9 × .... = 90
    d) .... × 9 = 45

    4 marks

4. a) 3 × 9 × 1 = ...
    b) 3 × 3 × 3 = ...

    2 marks

Now try these:

5. Work out the answers to these calculations.

    ```
       2 6            1 0 7
    ×    9          ×     9
    ———            ———
    ```

    ....

    2 marks

6. Austin is putting sweets into party bags.
    He puts 9 sweets in each party bag.
    He uses 81 sweets altogether.
    How many party bags does he make?

    ....

    1 mark

7. Sally-Anne the snail travels at a speed of 9 cm every minute. How long will it take her to reach a lettuce that is 36 cm away?

....
1 mark

8. Martin is moving 145 kg of sand from his driveway to a sandpit in his garden. He moves 10 kg of sand at a time. After he's made 9 trips he hurts his back and has to stop. How much sand is left to move?

....
2 marks

How did you do?   **Time:** [ ]   **Score:** [ ]

Puzzle: Poorly Piggy

Ady has got some medicine for his poorly pig, but he's forgotten which one is poorly.

Follow the clues below to find the number of the poorly pig.
Circle the pig that needs the medicine.

- It's bigger than 2 × 9 but smaller than 9 × 11.
- It's more than 9 times bigger than 5.
- If you divide it by 9, you'll get an answer bigger than 7.

Puzzle Complete?

© CGP — not to be photocopied   Autumn Term: Workout 3

Autumn Term: Workout 4

Quick fire

1. a) 2 × 3 = ...
    b) 9 × 8 = ...
    c) 11 × 4 = ...
    d) 12 × 6 = ...

    4 marks

2. a) 110 ÷ 11 = ...
    b) 24 ÷ 8 = ...
    c) 108 ÷ 9 = ...
    d) 27 ÷ 3 = ...

    4 marks

3. a) .... ÷ 8 = 8
    b) 12 × .... = 24
    c) .... × 11 = 77
    d) 56 ÷ .... = 8

    4 marks

4. a) What is ninety-six divided by eight? ....
    b) What is twelve times seven? ....

    2 marks

Now try these:

5. Mal's wand weighs 3 times more than Eric's wand. Eric's wand weighs 11 g. How much does Mal's weigh?

    ....
    1 mark

6. Glenn asks his 4 children to each carry 3 shopping bags. How many shopping bags do the children carry altogether?

    ....
    1 mark

7. Cecil's Suds charges £4.50 to clean a small car and £8.00 to clean a large car. How much money does Cecil's Suds charge for cleaning 1 small car and 6 large cars?

    ....
    2 marks

8. Frankie is making a video about his home town. He chooses 8 locations he wants to film in, and films for an equal amount of time in each place. When he's finished, he has 1 hour and 20 minutes of video. How many minutes did he spend filming in each location?

....
2 marks

How did you do?   Time:    Score:

Puzzle: Fun at the Fair

Some of the prices at a funfair are shown below.

Sarah has 3 turns on the Twirly-Whirly and 3 donkey rides. How much does she spend?

Donkey Rides £2
Twirly-Whirly £3
Super-Bungee £5
Mega-Fun Orbit £8
All Day Pass — Go on anything, as many times as you like! £50

....

Kika pays for her 6 children to go on the Twirly-Whirly. How much change does she get from £20?

....

Lee wants to have 3 turns on the Super-Bungee and 5 turns on the Mega-Fun Orbit. How much would he save if he bought an All Day Pass rather than paying for the rides individually?

....

Puzzle Complete?

Autumn Term: Workout 5

Quick fire

1. a) 5 × 11 = ...   c) 11 × 4 = ...

   b) 5 × 1 = ...   d) 11 × 12 = ...

   4 marks

2. a) 15 ÷ 5 = ...   c) 45 ÷ 9 = ...

   b) 33 ÷ 3 = ...   d) 11 ÷ 11 = ...

   4 marks

3. a) .... × 5 = 60   c) .... × 6 = 66

   b) 121 ÷ .... = 11   d) 40 ÷ .... = 8

   4 marks

4. a) 2 × 2 × 5 = ...   b) 2 × 11 × 3 = ...

   2 marks

Now try these:

5. Abdul is knitting socks for his baby brother.
   He needs 11 g of wool for each sock.
   How many socks can he knit with 110 g of wool?

   ....

   1 mark

6. Pene is handing out a bunch of daffodils to each person at a Mother's Day service. He has 100 bunches of daffodils. There are 8 rows of people, and 11 people on each row. How many bunches of daffodils will he have spare?

   ....

   2 marks

7. Mrs Morrison is pinning up 11 posters and 5 leaflets on the classroom wall. She uses 4 drawing pins to put up each poster, and 2 drawing pins to put up each leaflet. How many drawing pins will she need in total?

....
3 marks

How did you do?   Time: ☐   Score: ☐

Puzzle: Bath Time

Mari is going to bath her pets in weight order, from lightest to heaviest. Work out the weight of each pet in grams, then number them 1 to 5 to show the order that they'll be bathed in.

5 kg ÷ 10 = ...

5000 g ÷ 5 = ...

0.5 kg × 4 = ...

90 g × 11 = ...

500 g × 6 = ...

Puzzle Complete? ✓

Autumn Term: Workout 6

Quick fire

1. a) 11 × 6 = ...
    b) 6 × 2 = ...
    c) 6 × 3 = ...
    d) 4 × 7 = ...
    4 marks

2. a) 42 ÷ 7 = ...
    b) 30 ÷ 6 = ...
    c) 121 ÷ 11 = ...
    d) 84 ÷ 7 = ...
    4 marks

3. a) .... ÷ 11 = 9
    b) 6 × .... = 48
    c) 63 ÷ .... = 9
    d) .... ÷ 10 = 6
    4 marks

4. a) How many groups of five are in fifty-five? ....
    b) What is seven times seven? ....
    2 marks

Now try these:

5. a) Snappy the crocodile eats 6 birds a day. How many birds does he eat in a week?

    ....

    b) How many days does it take Snappy to eat 18 birds?

    ....
    2 marks

6. Eden is making lemonade. She needs 3 lemons to make 1 litre of lemonade. She has 21 lemons. How many litres of lemonade can she make?

    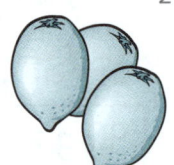

    ....
    1 mark

7. Adam recorded how many hours of sleep he got each night for a week. On 3 nights he got 7 hours of sleep and on 4 nights he got 6 hours of sleep.
How many hours of sleep did he get altogether?

....
3 marks

How did you do?   Time: Score:

Puzzle: Clowning Around

Trudy made a pictogram to show how many people she made laugh at different times of the day on Monday.

Key: 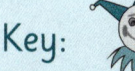 = 6 people

How many people did she make laugh in the afternoon?

....

In the evening she made 18 people laugh. Draw this information on the pictogram.

The same number of people laugh at Trudy every morning. How many days does it take for Trudy to make 36 people laugh in the morning?

....

Puzzle Complete?

Autumn Term: Workout 7

Quick fire

1. a) 9 × 5 = ...   c) 8 × 4 = ...
    b) 1 × 4 = ...   d) 9 × 3 = ...

    4 marks

2. a) 9 ÷ 9 = ...   c) 40 ÷ 4 = ...
    b) 72 ÷ 8 = ... d) 63 ÷ 7 = ...

    4 marks

3. a) .... × 4 = 20   c) .... ÷ 9 = 11
    b) 4 × .... = 44   d) 18 ÷ .... = 9

    4 marks

4. a) 2 × 2 × 3 = ...   b) 3 × 2 × 4 = ...

    2 marks

Now try these:

5. James has got to pump up each tyre on the school's 9 bicycles.
    How many tyres will he pump up altogether?

    ....
    1 mark

6. One teaspoon of sugar weighs 4 grams.
    There are 36 grams of sugar in Hallie's fizzy drink.
    How many teaspoons of sugar are there in the drink?

    ....
    1 mark

7. Amber makes a scrapbook using 36 photos.
    She puts 4 photos on each page. The scrapbook has 10 pages.
    How many pages won't have any photos?

    ....
    2 marks

8. Work out the answers to these calculations.

```
      ..........              ..........
   9 ⟌ 3 7 8             4 ⟌ 1 8 4
```

2 marks

How did you do?   **Time:** ☐   **Score:** ☐

Puzzle: Fluttering Around

The grid shows the starting position of 3 butterflies. Read the directions that each butterfly is going to fly in and then write down the coordinates of where they will land.

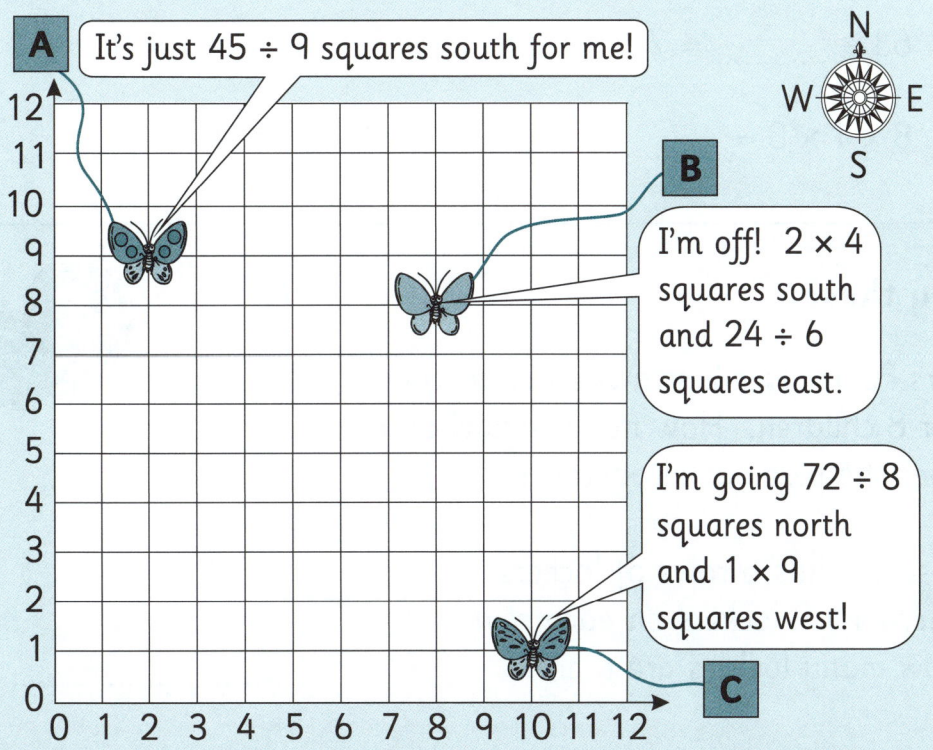

A: It's just 45 ÷ 9 squares south for me!

B: I'm off! 2 × 4 squares south and 24 ÷ 6 squares east.

C: I'm going 72 ÷ 8 squares north and 1 × 9 squares west!

Butterfly A: Butterfly B: Butterfly C:
(......... , ...)   (......... , ...)   (......... , ...)

Puzzle Complete?

Autumn Term: Workout 8

Quick fire

1. a) 9 × 10 = ...   c) 6 × 8 = ...

    b) 8 × 3 = ...   d) 9 × 12 = ...

    4 marks

2. a) 108 ÷ 12 = ...   c) 96 ÷ 8 = ...

    b) 45 ÷ 9 = ...   d) 8 ÷ 8 = ...

    4 marks

3. a) .... × 8 = 72   c) .... × 9 = 27

    b) 63 ÷ .... = 7   d) 32 ÷ .... = 8

    4 marks

4. a) 8 × 1 × 8 = ...   b) 2 × 11 × 4 ....

    2 marks

Now try these:

5. Mrs Polat gives 2 strawberries to each of her 8 children. How many strawberries does she give out altogether?   ....

    1 mark

6. A school has 6 rows of lockers. There are 9 lockers on each row. How many lockers are there?   ....

    1 mark

7. Mason received £4 from each of the 9 friends that came to his birthday party. He spent £12 of the money on a new hat. How much birthday money does Mason have left?

    ....

    2 marks

8. Lesley can get across his garden in 9 big jumps. To the nearest 10, how many jumps does it take him to get across his garden 9 times?

....
2 marks

How did you do? **Time:** ☐ **Score:** ☐

Puzzle: Cleaning Bonus!

Cleaners have been asked to clean the windows on the front of the building shown below.
Any cleaner that cleans 4 windows or more will get a bonus.

Which of these cleaners will get a bonus? Circle their name(s).

Rosie cleaned $\frac{1}{8}$ of the windows on the top floor.

Garret cleaned $\frac{1}{8}$ of the windows on the bottom floor.

Nelly cleaned $\frac{2}{9}$ of the windows on the middle floor.

Quentin cleaned $\frac{3}{8}$ of the windows on the bottom floor.

Puzzle Complete?

Autumn Term: Workout 9

Quick fire

1. a) 12 × 10 = ...   c) 6 × 4 = ...

    b) 9 × 6 = ...   d) 7 × 6 = ...

    4 marks

2. a) 144 ÷ 12 = ...   c) 14 ÷ 7 = ...

    b) 45 ÷ 9 = ...   d) 12 ÷ 1 = ...

    4 marks

3. a) .... × 7 = 84   c) 36 ÷ .... = 4

    b) 66 ÷ .... = 6   d) .... × 12 = 96

    4 marks

4. a) What is two divided by two? ....   b) What are two lots of eleven? ....

    2 marks

Now try these:

5. Work out the answers to these calculations.

    ```
        2 3 4              9 4 6
    ×       2          ×       6
    ─────────          ─────────
    ..........         ..........
    ```

    2 marks

6. Katie has bought 100 candles to decorate the tables at her wedding. She wants 8 candles on each of the 9 tables that her guests will sit at. The rest of the candles will go on her table. How many candles will be on Katie's table?

    ....

    2 marks

7. Jian has cooked 50 chicken nuggets for his son's party. He gives each child at the party 4 chicken nuggets and has 2 left over. How many children are at the party?

....
2 marks

How did you do?   Time: [ ]   Score: [ ]

Puzzle: Locked Boxes

Kevin the Kraken has four boxes and four keys. Each key opens a box with an equivalent multiplication on it. The answer to the multiplication tells you how many jewels are inside.

Work out which key opens each box and how many jewels each box contains.

Key A opens box .... It contains .... jewels.

Key B opens box .... It contains .... jewels.

Key C opens box .... It contains .... jewels.

Key D opens box .... It contains .... jewels.

Puzzle Complete?

Autumn Term: Workout 10

Quick fire

1. a) 2 × 11 = ...   c) 11 × 1 = ...
    b) 11 × 5 = ...   d) 4 × 11 = ...

    4 marks

2. a) 77 ÷ 11 = ...   c) 88 ÷ 11 = ...
    b) 99 ÷ 11 = ...   d) 55 ÷ 5 = ...

    4 marks

3. a) .... × 3 = 33   c) .... ÷ 11 = 6
    b) 121 ÷ .... = 11   d) .... × 11 = 11

    4 marks

4. a) What are ten lots of eleven? ....   b) How many lots of six make sixty-six? ....

    2 marks

Now try these:

5. Bobby rides her motorbike 4 times a day.
    She travels 11 kilometres on each ride.
    How many kilometres does Bobby ride in 2 days?

    ....

    2 marks

6. Daisy is planning to make some bird boxes for her garden.
    For each bird box she'll need 11 nails. She buys a pack of
    200 nails and works out that she'll have 68 nails left over.
    How many bird boxes is Daisy planning to make?

    ....

    2 marks

7. Fahim gets £2 a week from his grandmother, £2 a week from his dad and £5 a week from his mum. He saves all of the money. How much money will he save in 11 weeks?

....

2 marks

How did you do?   Time: ☐   Score: ☐

Puzzle: Harri's Hamsters

Harri's Pet Shop is due to get a delivery of baby hamsters. Harri's getting 11 cages ready for when they arrive. These are some of the things she's putting in each cage:

How many scoops of sawdust will Harri need for the new hamsters?

....

Harri only has 15 food bowls. How many more will she need?

....

The cardboard tubes come in packs of 10. How many packs of tubes will Harri need to buy?

....

Puzzle Complete?

Autumn Term: Workout 11

Quick fire

1. a) 12 × 9 = ...
   b) 5 × 10 = ...
   c) 10 × 8 = ...
   d) 7 × 12 = ...

   4 marks

2. a) 36 ÷ 4 = ...
   b) 36 ÷ 12 = ...
   c) 100 ÷ 10 = ...
   d) 24 ÷ 2 = ...

   4 marks

3. a) .... × 11 = 110
   b) 20 ÷ .... = 2
   c) 54 ÷ .... = 9
   d) .... × 1 = 12

   4 marks

4. a) What is double nine? ....
   b) What is sixty divided by ten? ....

   2 marks

Now try these:

5. Mr Costa is marking tests that his Year 5 class have done. He has 6 tests left to mark and there are 12 questions on each test. How many questions does he have left to mark?

   ....

   1 mark

6. Jill pays £4.75 each week for her phone contract. Raj pays £48 every 4 weeks for his phone contract. How much more expensive per week is Raj's phone contract than Jill's phone contract?

   ....

   2 marks

7. Maezah is making 7 fairy wands.
   a) She puts 9 hearts on each wand.
      How many hearts does she use? ....

   b) She puts 3 equal strands of ribbon on each wand.
      She uses 84 cm of ribbon in total. How many cm
      of ribbon does each wand have?
                                                 ....

   c) How long is each strand of ribbon? ....

   3 marks

How did you do?   **Time:** [ ]   **Score:** [ ]

Puzzle: Wendy's Potions

Wendy Witch is making potions.
She needs to add two ingredients to each cauldron.

- Draw lines to show which two ingredients she needs to put into each cauldron. She won't need to use all of the ingredients.
- Then work out the answers to the calculations on the cauldrons.

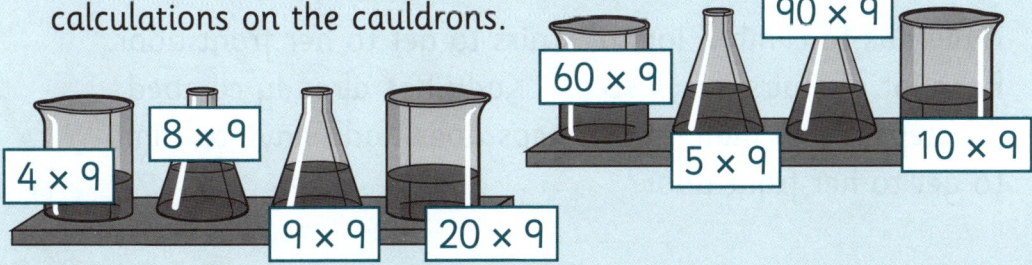

Try breaking the cauldron calculations into two easier calculations.

25 × 9

99 × 9

64 × 9

Puzzle Complete?

Autumn Term: Workout 11

Autumn Term: Workout 12

Quick fire

1. a) 11 × 4 = ... c) 9 × 2 = ...
   b) 7 × 8 = ... d) 9 × 8 = ...

   4 marks

2. a) 88 ÷ 11 = ... c) 132 ÷ 11 = ...
   b) 7 ÷ 1 = ... d) 24 ÷ 8 = ...

   4 marks

3. a) .... × 9 = 81 c) .... × 6 = 66
   b) 42 ÷ .... = 7 d) 27 ÷ .... = 3

   4 marks

4. a) 2 × 4 × 8 = ... b) 5 × 7 × 2 ....

   2 marks

Now try these:

5. Kady has to climb 7 lots of stairs to get to her front door. Each lot of stairs has 7 steps. Kady has already climbed 12 steps. How many more steps does Kady have to climb to get to her front door?

   ....

   2 marks

6. Monty is filling a shelf with tins of cat food. The shelf holds 9 rows of tins, with 7 tins in each row. So far he has put 30 tins on the shelf. How many more tins does he need to add to make the shelf full?

   ....

   2 marks

7. Work out the answers to these calculations.

$7\overline{)3\ 9\ 2}$ $8\overline{)1\ 2\ 8}$

2 marks

How did you do?   Time: Score:

Puzzle: Rachael's New Clothes!

Rachael Rabbit has bought herself 3 new tops and 7 new skirts.

How many different outfits made up of one top and one skirt can Rachael make from her new clothes? ....

Rachael owns 4 hats. How many different outfits made up of one top, one skirt and one hat can she make? ....

Rachael wears a different outfit (including a hat) every day. How many weeks' worth of outfits does she have?

....   **Puzzle Complete?**

Spring Term: Workout 1

Quick fire

1. a) 2 × 6 = ...
   b) 7 × 5 = ...
   c) 12 × 7 = ...
   d) 6 × 9 = ...

   4 marks

2. a) 21 ÷ 7 = ...
   b) 42 ÷ 6 = ...
   c) 56 ÷ 7 = ...
   d) 36 ÷ 6 = ...

   4 marks

3. a) 6 × .... = 18
   b) 63 ÷ .... = 7
   c) 7 × .... = 49
   d) 24 ÷ .... = 6

   4 marks

4. a) What is six times eight? ....
   b) How many sevens make fourteen? ....

   2 marks

Now try these:

5. a) Dan buys himself a coffee every day. One coffee costs £3. How much does Dan spend on coffee in one week?

   ....

   b) Dan is trying to reduce the amount of coffee he drinks. He starts buying tea instead of coffee every day apart from Sundays. One tea costs £2. How much does Dan spend on tea and coffee in one week now?

   ....

   3 marks

6. A supermarket sells apples in bags of six.
Lucy counts 11 bags of apples.
How many apples are there in total? ....

1 mark

7. a) Lucy wants to buy an apple for everyone in her class. There are 26 children in her class. How many bags of apples does she need to buy to make sure everyone gets one apple? ....

   b) How many apples will she have left over? ....

2 marks

How did you do?   Time: [   ]   Score: [   ]

Puzzle: Disco Dilemma

Vlad is attending a party at his friend's haunted mansion. Vlad loves to dance, but unfortunately for him the dancefloor has been booby-trapped. Only squares that can be divided by 6 or 7 are safe to dance on.
Colour in all the squares that Vlad can't dance on.

12	89	44	24	51
35	72	77	19	55
46	75	16	21	64
54	30	52	63	18
81	40	22	7	39

Puzzle Complete?

© CGP — not to be photocopied   Spring Term: Workout 1

Spring Term: Workout 2

Quick fire

1. a) 5 × 9 = ...   c) 6 × 12 = ...
   b) 10 × 11 = ...   d) 7 × 4 = ...

   4 marks

2. a) 36 ÷ 9 = ...   c) 80 ÷ 10 = ...
   b) 42 ÷ 7 = ...   d) 108 ÷ 12 = ...

   4 marks

3. a) 9 × .... = 63   c) 10 × .... = 20
   b) 84 ÷ .... = 7   d) 27 ÷ .... = 9

   4 marks

4. a) 4 × 2 × 10 = ...   b) 3 × 7 × 4 = ...

   2 marks

Now try these:

5. Josh bakes three trays of jam tarts.
   Each tray holds 12 tarts.
   How many jam tarts does Josh bake in total?   ....

   1 mark

6. Stuart owns 35 pairs of socks.
   He wears a fresh pair of socks every day.
   How many weeks can Stuart go before
   he needs to wash any of his socks?   ....

   1 mark

7. Zainab is 14 years old. She is twice the age
   of her brother Iqbal. Their sister Aisha is three
   times the age of Iqbal. How old is Aisha?

   ....

   2 marks

8. Pens are sold in packs of 20. Each pack contains
    10 black pens, 7 blue pens and 3 red pens.

    a) Max has bought 8 packs of pens.
       How many black pens has he bought? ....

    b) Seren has bought 24 red pens.
       How many packs of pens has she bought? ....

    2 marks

How did you do? **Time:** ☐ **Score:** ☐

Puzzle: How Old?

A group of friends work out their ages in months.
Draw a line from each of the friends to the birthday cake that
shows what their age in years will be on their next birthday.

Harriet	Charlie	Sean	Marcus	Evie

105 months	113 months	97 months	88 months	119 months

 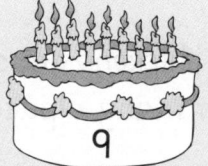 

8   9   10

Puzzle Complete?

Spring Term: Workout 3

Quick fire

1. a) 12 × 9 = ...
    b) 4 × 11 = ...
    c) 11 × 6 = ...
    d) 9 × 2 = ...

    4 marks

2. a) 88 ÷ 11 = ...
    b) 72 ÷ 9 = ...
    c) 22 ÷ 11 = ...
    d) 54 ÷ 9 = ...

    4 marks

3. a) 9 × .... = 99
    b) 33 ÷ .... = 3
    c) 11 × .... = 110
    d) 81 ÷ .... = 9

    4 marks

4. a) What is eleven lots of eleven? ....
    b) How many nines are in ninety? ....

    2 marks

Now try these:

5. The organisers of a football tournament are printing certificates for all the players that take part. There are eight teams in the tournament and eleven players on each team. How many certificates do they need to print?

    ....

    1 mark

6. On a farm, each group of 7 chickens are guarded by 2 alpacas. There are 63 chickens. How many alpacas are there?

    ....

    2 marks

7. Ethan and Steph are training for a bicycle race.
Ethan cycles 9 miles four times a week.
Steph cycles 11 miles twice a week.
How many more miles than Steph
does Ethan cycle in a week?

....
3 marks

How did you do?   **Time:**   **Score:**

Puzzle: A Game of Cards

At the end of a card game, the numbers on the five cards are added up. The winner must have a score that is a multiple of 9. If more than one player has a multiple of 9, the multiple that is the highest wins.

Work out the final score of each player below and circle the cards belonging to the winning player.

Puzzle Complete? ✓

Spring Term: Workout 4

Quick fire

1. a) 11 × 7 = ... c) 10 × 4 = ...
    b) 9 × 5 = ... d) 12 × 8 = ...

    4 marks

2. a) 60 ÷ 12 = ... c) 30 ÷ 10 = ...
    b) 70 ÷ 7 = ... d) 72 ÷ 12 = ...

    4 marks

3. a) 12 × .... = 48 c) 11 × .... = 132
    b) 50 ÷ .... = 10 d) 144 ÷ .... = 12

    4 marks

4. a) What is ten times seven? .... b) How many fives make twenty? ....

    2 marks

Now try these:

5. Ahmed is cooking pancakes. His recipe says that he needs 2 eggs to cook 12 pancakes. Ahmed wants to cook 84 pancakes. How many eggs will he need?

    ....

    2 marks

6. Elise is saving her pocket money to buy a computer game. The game costs £36. Elise has saved £3 a week for the past 7 weeks. How much more does she need to save?

    ....

    2 marks

7. Scarlett is icing some biscuits. She has 58 sweets to decorate the biscuits with and puts 5 sweets on each biscuit. When she has finished she has 3 sweets left over.
How many biscuits did Scarlett ice?

.... _____
                              2 marks

How did you do?   **Time:** [ ]   **Score:** [ ]

Puzzle: Ancient Amounts

Annie the Archaeologist is very excited. She's discovered a wax tablet belonging to an ancient Roman merchant. On the tablet, the merchant recorded everything he sold on one day.

Help Annie learn more about the merchant's business by doing the multiplication for her. Give your answers in Roman numerals.

= ....

= ....

= ....

= ....

Puzzle Complete?

Spring Term: Workout 5

Quick fire

1. a) 2 × 5 = ... c) 11 × 12 = ...
   b) 10 × 7 = ... d) 9 × 2 = ...

   4 marks

2. a) 84 ÷ 7 = ... c) 12 ÷ 12 = ...
   b) 20 ÷ 2 = ... d) 35 ÷ 7 = ...

   4 marks

3. a) 2 × .... = 22 c) 12 × .... = 72
   b) 28 ÷ .... = 7 d) 16 ÷ .... = 2

   4 marks

4. a) What are two lots of four? .... b) How many twelves make forty eight? ....

   2 marks

Now try these:

5. Work out the answers to these calculations.

   ```
     7 2            3 0 6
   ×   7          ×     2
   ───────        ───────
   ..........     ..........
   ```

   2 marks

6. How many days are there in seven weeks?

   ....

   1 mark

7. Barney's workshop has two rooms. The first room is a square with sides of length 12 m. The second room is rectangular with a length of 7 m and a width of 3 m. What is the total floor area of Barney's workshop?

.... _____
                         3 marks

How did you do?   **Time:** [   ]   **Score:** [   ]

Puzzle: At the Garden Centre

Agatha is buying some plants for her garden.
She wants 420 marigolds, 480 pansies and 240 geraniums.

Marigolds are sold in trays of 7, pansies are sold in trays of 12 and geraniums are sold in trays of 2.

Complete Agatha's shopping list by filling in how many trays of each plant she should buy.

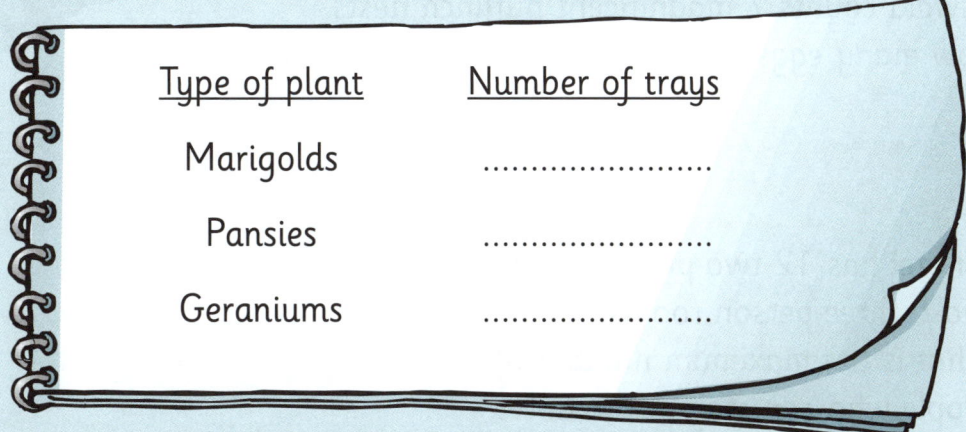

Type of plant	Number of trays
Marigolds	....
Pansies	....
Geraniums	....

Puzzle Complete?

Spring Term: Workout 6

Quick fire

1. a) 11 × 1 = ...   c) 5 × 5 = ...
   b) 3 × 12 = ...   d) 12 × 6 = ...

   4 marks

2. a) 99 ÷ 11 = ...   c) 30 ÷ 6 = ...
   b) 144 ÷ 12 = ...   d) 55 ÷ 5 = ...

   4 marks

3. a) 12 × .... = 24   c) 5 × .... = 15
   b) 66 ÷ .... = 11   d) 77 ÷ .... = 7

   4 marks

4. a) 5 × 6 × 2 = ... b) 11 × 4 × 2 = ...

   2 marks

Now try these:

5. Magnificent puffinches lay six eggs in their nests. Oswald counts 7 magnificent puffinch nests. How many eggs are there in total in these nests?

   .... *1 mark*

6. A hotel has 12 two-person rooms and 6 three-person rooms. What is the maximum number of people who can stay in the hotel?

   .... *3 marks*

7. Work out the answers to these calculations.

$$5\overline{)835} \qquad 6\overline{)564}$$

2 marks

How did you do?   **Time:** ☐   **Score:** ☐

Puzzle: At the Sweet Shop

Amy has £3 to spend. She visits the sweet shop.
She buys 8 foam mushrooms, 9 sugared almonds and 2 lollies.

How much money does Amy have left?
Give your answer in pounds.

....

Amy's sister Alice has £3 to spend. She spends it all on foam mushrooms. How many foam mushrooms does she buy?

....

Puzzle Complete?

Spring Term: Workout 7

Quick fire

1. a) 2 × 12 = ...
    b) 12 × 5 = ...
    c) 12 × 7 = ...
    d) 3 × 12 = ...
    4 marks

2. a) 48 ÷ 12 = ...
    b) 132 ÷ 12 = ...
    c) 36 ÷ 12 = ...
    d) 60 ÷ 12 = ...
    4 marks

3. a) 12 × .... = 12
    b) 84 ÷ .... = 12
    c) 12 × .... = 96
    d) 108 ÷ .... = 12
    4 marks

4. a) 2 × 4 × 12 = ...
    b) 12 × 3 × 3 = ...
    2 marks

Now try these:

5. In a park, there are 12 benches. 4 people can sit on each bench. Jia counts 35 people sitting on the benches. How many more people can sit on the benches?

    ....
    2 marks

6. In a bag containing pink and white sweets, there are 12 pink sweets. There are twice as many white sweets as pink sweets. What is the total number of sweets in the bag?

    ....
    2 marks

7. Eggs are sold in boxes of 12. Beryl the Baker needs 64 eggs. She buys 6 boxes of eggs. How many extra eggs will she have?

....
2 marks

How did you do?   Time: [ ]   Score: [ ]

Puzzle: Pie Proportions

Pythagoras runs a pie shop. He writes the amount of each pie sold each day as a fraction. Draw lines to match each fraction to the equivalent amount of pie sold.

Cheese and Onion $\dfrac{12}{48}$

Spinach and Mushroom $\dfrac{60}{72}$

Chicken Balti $\dfrac{12}{24}$

Rhubarb $\dfrac{24}{36}$

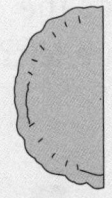 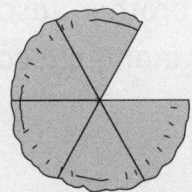 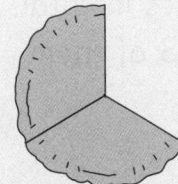 

Which pie has he sold the largest amount of?

....

Puzzle Complete?

Spring Term: Workout 8

Quick fire

1. a) 4 × 3 = ...   c) 3 × 9 = ...
   b) 7 × 5 = ...   d) 6 × 7 = ...

   4 marks

2. a) 21 ÷ 3 = ...   c) 49 ÷ 7 = ...
   b) 14 ÷ 7 = ...   d) 30 ÷ 3 = ...

   4 marks

3. a) 12 × .... = 36   c) 7 × .... = 56
   b) 18 ÷ .... = 3   d) 63 ÷ .... = 7

   4 marks

4. a) What is two lots of three? ....
   b) How many sevens make seventy seven? ....

   2 marks

Now try these:

5. Jasmine has baked some cupcakes. She stores them in boxes of 4 and fills 7 boxes in total. Her brother Jason finds the cupcakes and eats 3 of them. How many cupcakes are left?

   2 marks

6. Olufemi's teacher says that there are 3 hours and 40 minutes until hometime. How many minutes are there until hometime?

   2 marks

7. Barbara and Doris are both knitting scarves. Barbara's scarf is 12 cm long. Doris's scarf is 72 cm longer than Barbara's. How many times longer than Barbara's scarf is Doris's scarf?

....
2 marks

How did you do?   Time: ☐   Score: ☐

Puzzle: Football Figures

Francesca is the captain of a football team. She's produced a bar chart of their results last season, which is shown below. Unfortunately, she forgot to add a scale!

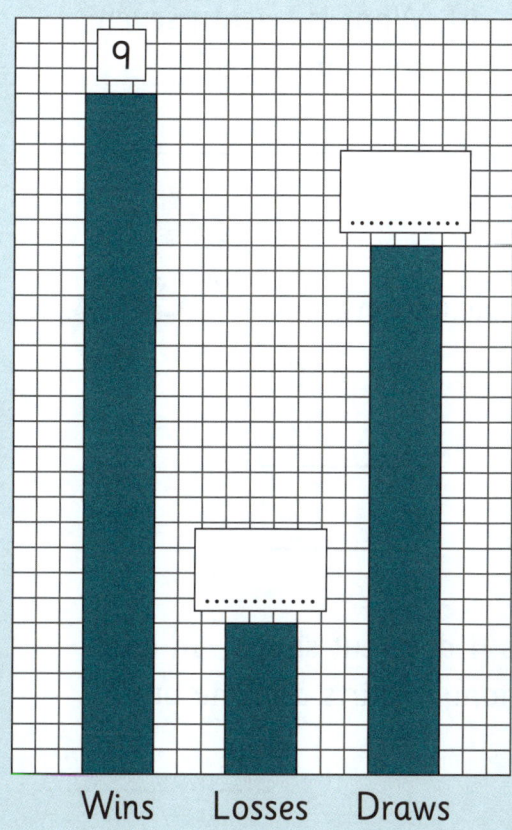

a) The team won 9 of their matches last season. Work out how many matches they lost and how many matches they drew. Write the numbers above the bars on the chart.

b) Teams get 3 points for a win, 1 point for a draw, and no points for a loss. How many points did Francesca's team get last year?

....

Puzzle Complete?

Spring Term: Workout 9

Quick fire

1. a) 4 × 4 = ...   c) 3 × 3 = ...
    b) 11 × 5 = ...   d) 4 × 5 = ...
    4 marks

2. a) 36 ÷ 3 = ...   c) 48 ÷ 4 = ...
    b) 24 ÷ 3 = ...   d) 88 ÷ 11 = ...
    4 marks

3. a) 4 × .... = 36   c) 3 × .... = 21
    b) 28 ÷ .... = 4   d) 66 ÷ .... = 11
    4 marks

4. a) What is four times eight? ....   b) What is twenty seven split into three? ....
    2 marks

Now try these:

5. Work out the answers to these calculations.

    ```
       3 3           2 4 0
    ×    7         ×     4
    ------         -------
    ```
    ....
    2 marks

6. Harvey goes shopping. He visits 4 different shops. In each shop he buys 3 T-shirts. How many T-shirts does he buy?

    ....
    1 mark

7. a) A hockey team is made up of 11 players.
        The Haverrow Hooligans Hockey Club has 39 members.
        How many teams can they send to the next tournament?

        ....

    b) How many more members would the Haverrow Hooligans
        need to send one more team to the tournament?

        ....

        3 marks

How did you do?   **Time:** [ ]   **Score:** [ ]

Puzzle: Pizza Possibilities

Katja is ordering some pizzas.
Here are the options available:

Cheese	Topping
• Mozzarella	• Pineapple
• Cheddar	• Pepperoni
• Goat's	• Mushroom
• Vegan	• Tuna
	• Ham
	• Peppers

How many different pizzas with one type of cheese and one topping could Katja order?

....

Katja will be sharing the pizzas with 5 friends. She wants to make sure everyone gets at least four slices. Each pizza has 8 slices. What is the smallest number of pizzas Katja can buy?

....

Puzzle Complete?

Spring Term: Workout 9

Spring Term: Workout 10

Quick fire

1. a) 8 × 7 = ...   c) 5 × 3 = ...
   b) 6 × 11 = ... d) 5 × 9 = ...

   4 marks

2. a) 64 ÷ 8 = ... c) 60 ÷ 5 = ...
   b) 27 ÷ 9 = ... d) 56 ÷ 8 = ...

   4 marks

3. a) 8 × .... = 48   c) 9 × .... = 36
   b) 22 ÷ .... = 11 d) 25 ÷ .... = 5

   4 marks

4. a) What is two lots of eight? ....   b) How many nines are in eighteen? ....

   2 marks

Now try these:

5. a) Tatenda is filling party bags to give to the guests at her birthday party. There are 9 guests and she wants to put 3 stickers in each bag. Stickers come in packs of 8. How many packets of stickers does Tatenda need to buy to make sure she has enough?

   ....

   b) How many stickers does Tatenda have left over?

   ....

   3 marks

6. An individual packet of brussels sprout crisps costs 11p. In a multipack containing 6 packets, each packet is worth 8p. Obi wants five packets of crisps. How much cheaper is it to buy the multipack than to buy 5 individual packets?

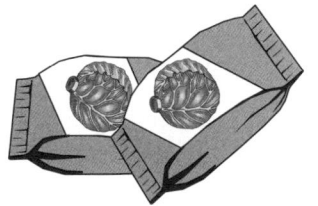

....
———————
3 marks

How did you do?   **Time:**   **Score:**

Puzzle: Humphrey's Hats

Humphrey is tidying his hat collection. He keeps two hats in each box, but they can't be any two hats. The numbers on the hats must add up to the answer to the calculation shown on the box. Draw lines to show which hats go in each box.

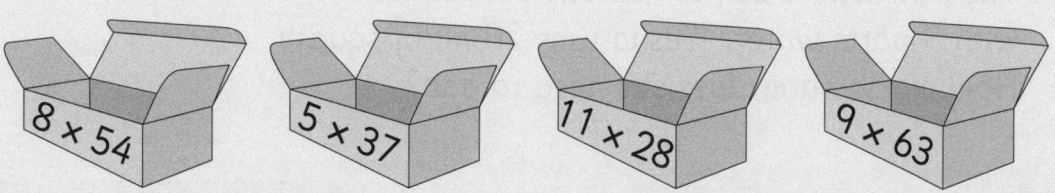

Puzzle Complete?

Spring Term: Workout 11

Quick fire

1. a) 6 × 5 = ...   c) 9 × 9 = ...
   b) 8 × 9 = ...   d) 6 × 6 = ...

   4 marks

2. a) 90 ÷ 9 = ...   c) 6 ÷ 6 = ...
   b) 66 ÷ 6 = ...   d) 45 ÷ 9 = ...

   4 marks

3. a) 9 × .... = 63   c) 9 × .... = 108
   b) 27 ÷ .... = 9   d) 72 ÷ .... = 6

   4 marks

4. a) 6 × 9 × 2 = ...   b) 4 × 6 × 3 = ...

   2 marks

Now try these:

5. Omar cuts 6 apples into quarters.
   He eats 7 of the quarters.
   How many pieces of apple does he have left?

   2 marks

6. Sasha is making a glass of orange squash.
   The instructions say to mix one part squash
   with 9 parts water. Sasha uses 20 ml of squash.
   How much water does she need to add?

   2 marks

7. A group of 36 people are waiting to go on a ride at a theme park. 9 people can go on the ride at once. The ride lasts 6 minutes. How long will it take for all 36 people to go on the ride?

....

2 marks

How did you do?   **Time:** ☐   **Score:** ☐

Puzzle: Finley's Special Punch

Finley has a punch recipe for 6 people, but he wants to make as much punch as possible using 18 cups of tomato juice.

Complete the recipe to show how many people Finley can make punch for using 18 cups of tomato juice, and how much of each of the other ingredients he'll need.

Special punch for 6 people

3 cups lemonade

2 cups tomato juice

5 teaspoons maple syrup

4 teaspoons cinnamon

7 drops peppermint extract

12 glacé cherries

Special punch for .... people

.... cups lemonade

18 cups tomato juice

.... teaspoons maple syrup

.... teaspoons cinnamon

.... drops peppermint extract

.... glacé cherries

Puzzle Complete?

Spring Term: Workout 12

Quick fire

1. a) 4 × 2 = ...
   b) 6 × 9 = ...
   c) 4 × 11 = ...
   d) 10 × 2 = ...

   4 marks

2. a) 77 ÷ 11 = ...
   b) 6 ÷ 2 = ...
   c) 99 ÷ 9 = ...
   d) 18 ÷ 2 = ...

   4 marks

3. a) 2 × .... = 2
   b) 12 ÷ .... = 2
   c) 11 × .... = 88
   d) 9 ÷ .... = 1

   4 marks

4. a) What is eleven times five? ....
   b) What is half of sixteen? ....

   2 marks

Now try these:

5. 9 pupils from each class take part in a school sports day. There are 4 year groups in the school and 2 classes in each year. How many pupils in total take part in the sports day?

   ....

   2 marks

6. A beaver can cut down 9 trees in 11 days. How many trees can it cut down in 33 days?

   ....

   2 marks

7. Work out the answers to these calculations.

$$2 \overline{) 7\ 5\ 2} \qquad 9 \overline{) 2\ 4\ 3}$$

2 marks

How did you do? Time: ☐ Score: ☐

Puzzle: Present Problems

Saoirse is wrapping some presents. Each present has sides of equal length. Saoirse wants to tie a ribbon around each present. The length of the ribbon must be equal to the distance around the outside of the present, plus 30 cm to tie the bow.
Draw lines to match each present to the correct length ribbon.

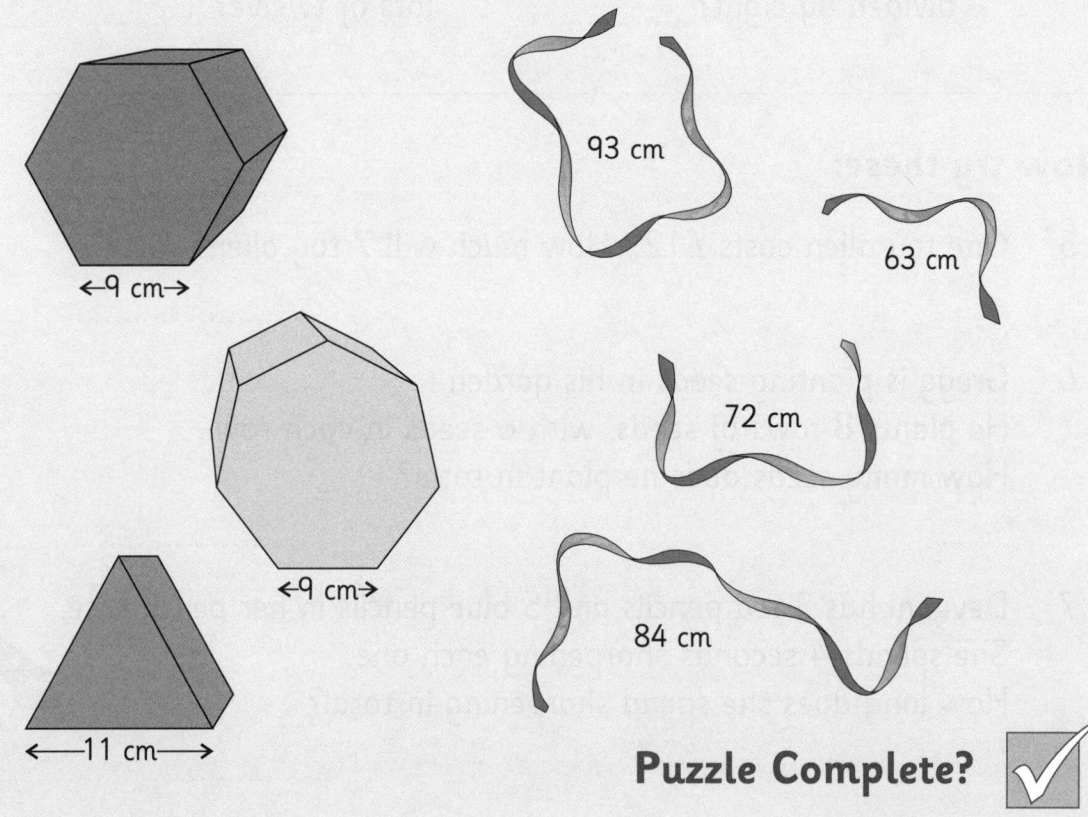

Puzzle Complete? ✓

Summer Term: Workout 1

Quick fire

1. a) 2 × 8 = ...
   b) 3 × 12 = ...
   c) 11 × 8 = ...
   d) 4 × 12 = ...

   4 marks

2. a) 144 ÷ 12 = ...
   b) 60 ÷ 12 = ...
   c) 56 ÷ 8 = ...
   d) 80 ÷ 8 = ...

   4 marks

3. a) .... × 8 = 64
   b) 12 × .... = 132
   c) .... ÷ 12 = 10
   d) 12 ÷ .... = 1

   4 marks

4. a) What is forty-eight divided by eight? ....
   b) What are nine lots of twelve? ....

   2 marks

Now try these:

5. One toy alien costs £12. How much will 7 toy aliens cost?

   ....

   1 mark

6. Gregg is planting seeds in his garden.
   He plants 8 rows of seeds, with 6 seeds in each row.
   How many seeds does he plant in total?

   ....

   1 mark

7. Devyani has 3 red pencils and 5 blue pencils in her pencil case.
   She spends 4 seconds sharpening each one.
   How long does she spend sharpening in total?

   ....

   2 marks

8. In class 5, every time a child gets a gold star for their work they earn 8 points for the class. When the class have earned 250 points they will get a prize. So far the class have earned 210 points. How many more children need to get a gold star for the class to get a prize?

....

2 marks

How did you do?   Time: ☐   Score: ☐

Puzzle: New Ferry!

Fred's Ferries have bought a new boat to carry people to an island in the middle of Lake Gustemere. The old boat could carry 8 people at a time, but the new boat can carry 12 people at a time.

Look at the groups below. Write down how many journeys each boat would have to make to take all the people in each group from the lakeshore to the island.

Year 4 trip from local school — 24 children

Coachload of tourists — 72 people

Open-air concert audience — 96 people

old boat ....

new boat ....

Puzzle Complete? ✓

Summer Term: Workout 2

Quick fire

1. a) 3 × 4 = ...   c) 12 × 6 = ...
    b) 5 × 11 = ...   d) 8 × 7 = ...

    4 marks

2. a) 77 ÷ 11 = ... c) 54 ÷ 6 = ...
    b) 48 ÷ 4 = ...   d) 49 ÷ 7 = ...

    4 marks

3. a) .... × 7 = 21   c) .... ÷ 7 = 10
    b) .... ÷ 11 = 12 d) 6 × .... = 24

    4 marks

4. a) What is six times by eight? ....
    b) How many elevens make sixty-six? ....

    2 marks

Now try these:

5. One envelope weighs 7 grams. How much do 9 envelopes weigh?

    ....

    1 mark

6. Theo buys 11 chocolate biscuits for 99p. How much does each chocolate biscuit cost?

    ....

    1 mark

7. Michael has a 50 ml bottle of hand gel. He uses 4 ml a day. How much will he have left after 7 days?

    ....

    2 marks

8. Verity has been given a box of bandages, so she decides to play hospitals with her 6 teddies. She puts 3 bandages on each teddy and leaves 3 bandages in the box. How many bandages were in the box to start with?

....
2 marks

How did you do?   Time: [ ]   Score: [ ]

Puzzle: Under the Sea

The Midsea Merpeople are having a competition. Each merperson has to collect a shell from the bottom of the sea. Each shell is then weighed, and the one with the closest weight to the Merking's Magic Rock is the winner. Circle the winning shell below.

Puzzle Complete?

Summer Term: Workout 3

Quick fire

1. a) 12 × 3 = ...
    b) 11 × 7 = ...
    c) 2 × 10 = ...
    d) 7 × 3 = ...
    4 marks

2. a) 84 ÷ 7 = ...
    b) 120 ÷ 10 = ...
    c) 33 ÷ 3 = ...
    d) 49 ÷ 7 = ...
    4 marks

3. a) .... × 7 = 42
    b) 12 ÷ .... = 3
    c) .... × 10 = 50
    d) 18 ÷ .... = 3
    4 marks

4. a) 2 × 10 × 3 = ...
    b) 5 × 11 × 2 ....
    2 marks

Now try these:

5. Ray's bathroom floor has 9 rows of tiles, with 10 tiles in each row. How many tiles are on Ray's bathroom floor?

    ....
    1 mark

6. Honnesh threw his ball 3 metres across a field. Mary threw her ball 3 times further than Honnesh threw his. How far across the field did Mary throw her ball?

    ....
    1 mark

7. Sabine eats 4 pieces of fruit a day. How many pieces of fruit does she eat in 10 weeks?

    ....
    2 marks

8. There are 27 children in Mr Wilson's class.
   On Monday, $\frac{1}{3}$ of the children didn't wear their school jumper.

   How many children in Mr Wilson's class **did** wear their school jumper on Monday?

....
2 marks

How did you do?   **Time:** [   ]   **Score:** [   ]

Puzzle: Sale Time!

A gadget shop is having a sale. The price tag on each item shows its original price. Complete the poster below to show how much each item costs in the sale.

Puzzle Complete?

Summer Term: Workout 4

Quick fire

1. a) 5 × 12 = ...
   b) 6 × 3 = ...
   c) 7 × 4 = ...
   d) 7 × 3 = ...

   4 marks

2. a) 108 ÷ 12 = ...
   b) 44 ÷ 4 = ...
   c) 30 ÷ 3 = ...
   d) 96 ÷ 12 = ...

   4 marks

3. a) .... × 4 = 24
   b) 132 ÷ .... = 11
   c) .... × 3 = 21
   d) 40 ÷ .... = 10

   4 marks

4. a) 2 × 1 × 12 = ...
   b) 7 × 3 × 4 = ...

   2 marks

Now try these:

5. Work out the answers to these calculations.

   ```
       4 8 5           1 9 8
   ×       4       ×       3
   ─────────       ─────────
   ..........      ..........
   ```

   2 marks

6. Caetlin is making a playlist of her favourite songs. Each song is 3 minutes long. So far her playlist is 15 minutes long. How many songs does she have on her playlist so far?

   ....

   1 mark

7. Marlee has 4 cats. She buys a packet of 50 cat biscuits.
Every day she gives each cat 3 biscuits.
How many biscuits will she have left after 3 days?

....
3 marks

How did you do?   Time: ☐   Score: ☐

Puzzle: Mrs Vasso's Art Wall

Mrs Vasso asked some children to draw their favourite animals.
Work out the area of each of the children's drawings below.
All measurements shown are in inches (in).

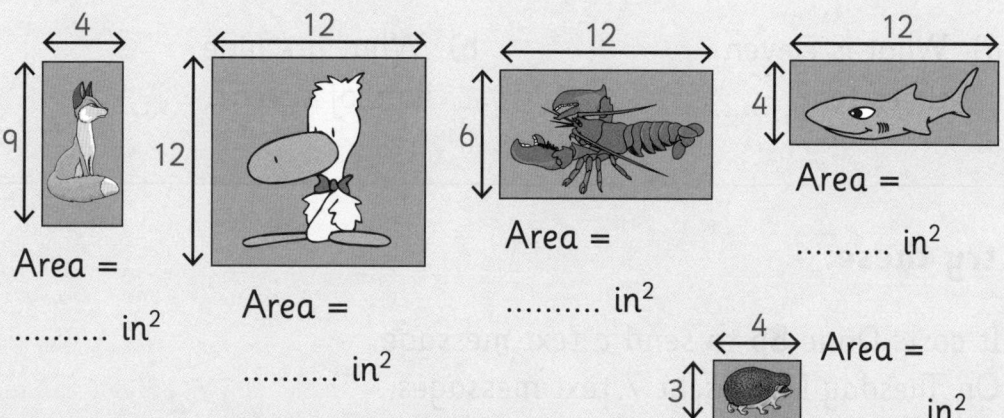

Mrs Vasso is going to display some of the drawings on her art wall. Her art wall is 3 metres long and 1 metre high. What is the area of Mrs Vasso's art wall?

.... m²

Mrs Vasso puts the 3 largest drawings side by side on the wall. What length of the wall do these drawings cover in inches?

....

Puzzle Complete?

Summer Term: Workout 5

Quick fire

1. a) 2 × 11 = ...
   b) 12 × 7 = ...
   c) 9 × 6 = ...
   d) 3 × 6 = ...
   4 marks

2. a) 96 ÷ 8 = ...
   b) 28 ÷ 7 = ...
   c) 48 ÷ 6 = ...
   d) 121 ÷ 11 = ...
   4 marks

3. a) .... × 11 = 44
   b) .... ÷ 11 = 8
   c) .... ÷ 7 = 6
   d) 8 × .... = 72
   4 marks

4. a) What is eleven times ten? ....
   b) What are nine lots of seven? ....
   2 marks

Now try these:

5. It costs Dane 8p to send a text message.
   On Tuesday Dane sent 7 text messages.
   How much did Dane spend on text messages on Tuesday?

   ....
   1 mark

6. Skylar is building a tower out of foam bricks. Each brick is 11 cm high. She wants her tower to be at least 1 metre tall. What is the lowest number of bricks she needs to use?

   ....
   2 marks

7. Mrs Alberry is paying for her 5 children to go to a play centre and then to the cinema. Altogether Mrs Alberry spends £70. Each cinema ticket costs £6.
   How much does each play centre ticket cost?

   ....

   3 marks

   How did you do?   Time: [ ]   Score: [ ]

   Puzzle: Connie's Coconuts

   Connie the monkey is swinging through the trees to get some coconuts. She can only swing between trees that are prime numbers. Draw a path that Connie could take.

   The number of coconuts Connie will get is a prime number less than 10 and a factor of 24. How many coconuts might Connie get? Write down all the possible answers.

   ....   **Puzzle Complete?**

Summer Term: Workout 6

Quick fire

1. a) 5 × 7 = ... c) 9 × 7 = ...

   b) 1 × 7 = ... d) 4 × 7 = ...

   4 marks

2. a) 77 ÷ 7 = ... c) 84 ÷ 7 = ...

   b) 49 ÷ 7 = ... d) 56 ÷ 7 = ...

   4 marks

3. a) .... × 7 = 70 c) .... ÷ 7 = 1

   b) .... ÷ 7 = 2 d) 7 × .... = 42

   4 marks

4. a) What is seventy shared by seven? ....   b) What are eleven lots of seven? ....

   2 marks

Now try these:

5. Work out the answers to these calculations.

   7) 2 8 4 9   7) 5 8 4

   2 marks

6. Tanya did a survey to find out what colour socks people were wearing in her school. The pictogram below shows her results.

   Black 🧦🧦🧦🧦🧦🧦   🧦 = 7 people
   Blue 🧦🧦
   White 🧦🧦🧦🧦

   How many people were in Tanya's survey?

   ....

   1 mark

7. Mr Greenfingers has 6 sunflower plants and 9 pea plants. Every morning he gives each plant 7 millilitres of water. How many millilitres of water does he need for all of his plants each morning?

....

3 marks

How did you do?   Time: ☐   Score: ☐

Puzzle: Story Book Characters

Vishnu has found information about three of his favourite story book characters.

Name: Mr Bleugh
Weight: 2 kilograms
Height: 14 inches

Name: Silver Crusader
Weight: 1500 kilograms
Height: 7 metres and 15 centimetres

Name: Lil Ratto
Weight: 7 kilograms
Height: 17 centimetres

Use these conversions to help you answer the questions below.

1 metre ≈ 3 feet
5 centimetres ≈ 2 inches
1 kilogram ≈ 2 pounds

('≈' means 'about equal to')

What is Lil Ratto's weight in pounds? .... pounds

What is Mr Bleugh's height in centimetres? .... centimetres

What is Silver Crusader's height in feet and inches?
.... feet and .... inches

Puzzle Complete?

Summer Term: Workout 7

Quick fire

1. a) 4 × 6 = ...   c) 7 × 9 = ...
    b) 11 × 3 = ... d) 4 × 12 = ...

    4 marks

2. a) 63 ÷ 7 = ... c) 22 ÷ 11 = ...
    b) 20 ÷ 4 = ... d) 54 ÷ 9 = ...

    4 marks

3. a) 9 × .... = 18   c) 10 × .... = 110
    b) 28 ÷ .... = 4   d) 16 ÷ .... = 4

    4 marks

4. a) 2 × 4 × 7 = ... b) 3 × 3 × 9 = ...

    2 marks

Now try these:

5. Charlie has 4 dogs. Every day he feeds them 2 treats each.
    Charlie buys a bag of 88 treats.
    How many days will the bag last?

    2 marks

6. Freya has been keeping a diary for exactly 5 weeks.
    She writes one page in her diary every day.
    The diary has 60 pages. How many blank pages are left?

    2 marks

7. Stan is a car park security guard. He walks around the perimeter of the car park 9 times during his shift. The car park is a square with sides of 100 m. How far does Stan walk during his shift?

....
2 marks

How did you do?   **Time:**   **Score:**

Puzzle: Hattie's Tea Party

Hattie is trying to find 4 matching cups from her collection to use at a tea party. The calculations on the 4 cups all have the same remainder. Help Hattie by circling the matching cups.

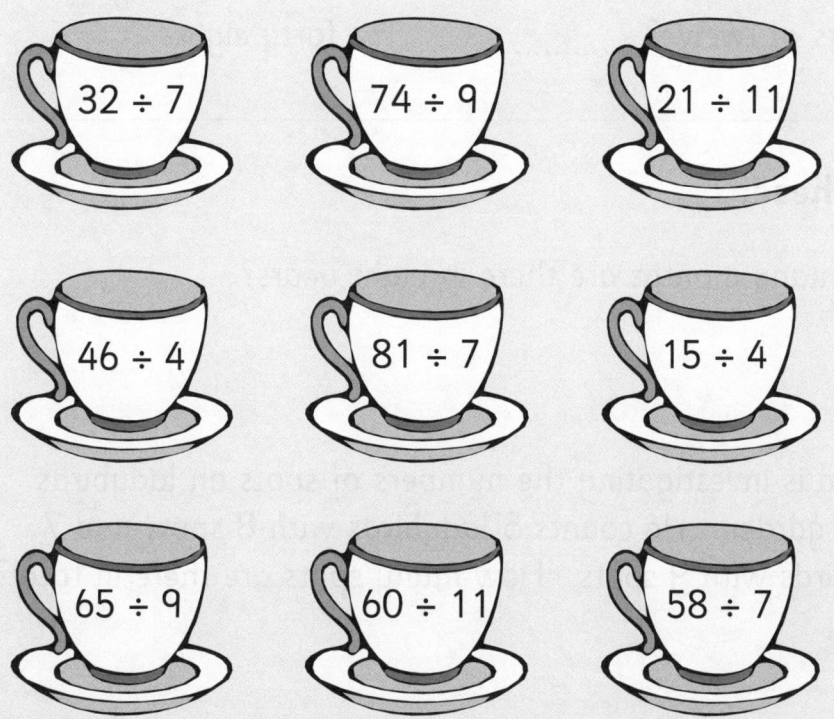

Puzzle Complete?

Summer Term: Workout 8

Quick fire

1. a) 6 × 9 = ... c) 8 × 3 = ...
   b) 12 × 7 = ... d) 11 × 12 = ...

   4 marks

2. a) 12 ÷ 6 = ... c) 72 ÷ 8 = ...
   b) 24 ÷ 12 = ... d) 36 ÷ 9 = ...

   4 marks

3. a) 8 × .... = 40 c) 9 × .... = 81
   b) 36 ÷ .... = 12 d) 18 ÷ .... = 6

   4 marks

4. a) What are nine lots of twelve? ....
   b) How many eights make forty eight? ....

   2 marks

Now try these:

5. How many months are there in eight years?

   .... *1 mark*

6. Rashid is investigating the numbers of spots on ladybirds in his garden. He counts 5 ladybirds with 8 spots and 7 ladybirds with 9 spots. How many spots are there in total?

   .... *3 marks*

7. Work out the answers to these calculations.

```
    1 2 1 4              7 5
  ×       6          ×   1 2
  ─────────          ─────────
  .........          +
                     ─────────

                     .........
```
2 marks

How did you do?   **Time:** [ ]   **Score:** [ ]

Puzzle: Ted's in Trouble

It's Ted's first day working in a nursery. He needs to give the babies their bottles, but he's forgotten whose is whose.

The babies and bottles are labelled with factor pairs. Draw a line from each baby to its correct bottle by matching factor pairs of the same number.

Puzzle Complete?

Summer Term: Workout 9

Quick fire

1. a) 12 × 6 = ...   c) 7 × 6 = ...
    b) 6 × 8 = ...   d) 6 × 9 = ...

    4 marks

2. a) 72 ÷ 6 = ...   c) 6 ÷ 6 = ...
    b) 66 ÷ 6 = ...   d) 12 ÷ 6 = ...

    4 marks

3. a) 6 × .... = 24   c) 6 × .... = 60
    b) 36 ÷ .... = 6   d) 30 ÷ .... = 6

    4 marks

4. a) What is four times six? ....   b) How many sixes are in eighteen? ....

    2 marks

Now try these:

5. Ava shares 48 radishes equally between her six rabbits. How many radishes does each rabbit get?

   ....

   1 mark

6. A café sells 6 cheese sandwiches for every 5 egg sandwiches sold. One lunchtime, the café sells 15 egg sandwiches. How many cheese sandwiches does it sell?

   ....

   2 marks

7. Gary the grasshopper is 6 cm long. He jumps 4 times, moving in a straight line. Each jump is 20 times his body length. How far does he travel?

....
3 marks

How did you do? **Time:** ☐ **Score:** ☐

Puzzle: How Far?

Snoozeton council has put some new road signs in the town. But there's a problem. All the distances have been written as fractions and it's confusing people! The council want to change the signs to show the distances as mixed numbers. Write down the mixed numbers the new signs need to show.

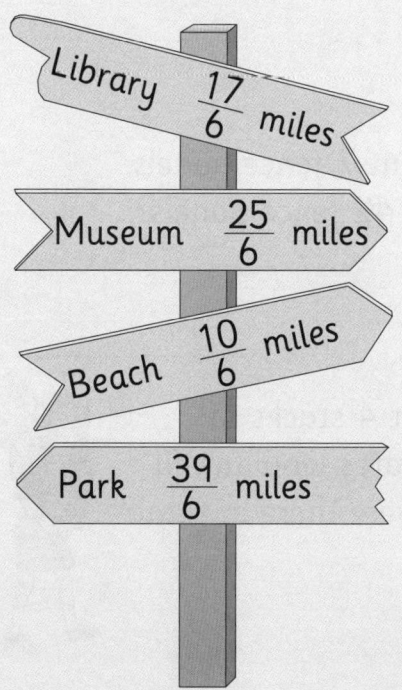

Library .... miles

Museum .... miles

Beach .... miles

Park .... miles

Puzzle Complete?

Summer Term: Workout 10

Quick fire

1. a) 10 × 5 = ...   c) 11 × 8 = ...
    b) 12 × 7 = ...   d) 2 × 10 = ...

    4 marks

2. a) 80 ÷ 10 = ...   c) 96 ÷ 8 = ...
    b) 14 ÷ 7 = ...   d) 32 ÷ 8 = ...

    4 marks

3. a) 8 × .... = 16   c) 10 × .... = 40
    b) 28 ÷ .... = 7   d) 120 ÷ .... = 10

    4 marks

4. a) 3 × 10 × 2 = ...   b) 2 × 5 × 10 = ...

    2 marks

Now try these:

5. Tom is painting a fence.
   One tub contains enough paint to paint 7 fence panels.
   How many tubs will he need to paint 42 fence panels?

   ....
   1 mark

6. Lily tidied away some plates. She put 4 stacks of 10 plates each into a cupboard. 6 plates wouldn't fit in the cupboard. How many plates were there in total?

   ....
   2 marks

7. Euan does 8 star jumps every day for a week.
   The next week he does 9 star jumps every day.
   How many star jumps does he do in total over the 2 weeks?

....
3 marks

How did you do?   Time: [ ]   Score: [ ]

Puzzle: Which Keys?

Persie the pirate is checking up on her 4 chests of loot.
To open each chest, she needs to use two keys.

For each pair of keys, subtracting the answer to the calculation on one key from the answer to the calculation on the other key gives the number of the chest that they open.

Draw lines to match the keys to the correct chests.

Puzzle Complete? ✓

Summer Term: Workout 11

Quick fire

1. a) 3 × 7 = ...   c) 8 × 11 = ...
   b) 10 × 5 = ... d) 7 × 7 = ...

   4 marks

2. a) 70 ÷ 7 = ... c) 10 ÷ 10 = ...
   b) 24 ÷ 8 = ... d) 40 ÷ 8 = ...

   4 marks

3. a) 7 × .... = 84   c) 10 × .... = 60
   b) 72 ÷ .... = 8   d) 56 ÷ .... = 7

   4 marks

4. a) What are ten lots of nine? ....
   b) How many sevens make thirty five? ....

   2 marks

Now try these:

5. Work out the answers to these calculations.

   7) 2737   9) 489

   2 marks

6. Hair bands come in packs of 12.
   Each pack costs £2. Anjali spent £6 on hair bands.
   How many hair bands did she buy?

   2 marks

7. On a packet of seeds, Ruby reads that 9 out of every 12 seeds should sprout. Ruby plants 72 seeds. How many should she expect to sprout?

....
2 marks

How did you do? Time: ☐ Score: ☐

Puzzle: Add Up the Scores

In a quiz, players get 5 points for a correct answer to a question but lose 2 points for an incorrect answer. The table below shows how many questions each player answered, and how many of those questions they answered correctly and incorrectly.

Look at each row of the table and work out the missing numbers for each player.

Name	Questions Answered	Correct Answers	Incorrect Answers	Points
Amir	12	5	7	....
Rosie	11	9	2	....
Inaya	....	8	5	....
Lily-Mae	12	....	3	....
Charles	13	7	....	....

Puzzle Complete?

Summer Term: Workout 12

Quick fire

1. a) 5 × 12 = ...
    b) 4 × 9 = ...
    c) 7 × 4 = ...
    d) 3 × 5 = ...

    4 marks

2. a) 7 ÷ 7 = ...
    b) 24 ÷ 12 = ...
    c) 55 ÷ 5 = ...
    d) 18 ÷ 9 = ...

    4 marks

3. a) 12 × .... = 48
    b) 27 ÷ .... = 9
    c) 5 × .... = 35
    d) 42 ÷ .... = 7

    4 marks

4. a) What are eleven lots of twelve? ....
    b) How many fives make twenty five? ....

    2 marks

Now try these:

5. Madison works for 9 hours a day. How many hours does she work in 5 days?

    ....

    1 mark

6. Fatima can unicycle 9 miles in an hour. One day she unicycles 27 miles. Steve unicycles 15 miles in the same time. How far could Steve unicycle in an hour?

    ....

    2 marks

7. Jayden is doing a sponsored swim. He has 7 sponsors.
   4 of his sponsors give him £5 and 3 give him £12.
   How much money does Jayden raise in total?

....

3 marks

How did you do?   Time: [   ]   Score: [   ]

Puzzle: Say Cheese

Some mice took part in a cheese-eating contest.
The fraction of a whole cheese eaten by each mouse is shown below. Number the mice from 1-5 to show the order in which they came in the contest. The mouse that ate the most cheese came first and the mouse that ate the least cheese came fifth.

It's much easier to compare the sizes of fractions when their denominators are the same.

Squeaker $\frac{16}{36}$

Enor Mouse $\frac{24}{72}$

Julius Cheeser
$\frac{5}{45}$

Anonymouse $\frac{42}{54}$

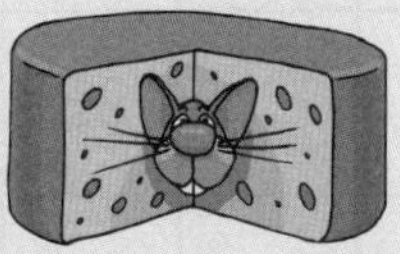

Fay Mouse
$\frac{16}{18}$

Puzzle Complete? ✓

Times Tables Chart

Fill in the missing numbers in the multiplication chart below to show all of the times tables.

×	1	2	3	4	5	6	7	8	9	10	11	12
1	1											
2												
3					15							
4		8										
5										50		
6												
7												
8												
9												
10												120
11			33									
12												

Times Tables Chart

Autumn Term

Workout 1 — pages 2-3

1. a) **25** 1 mark   c) **24** 1 mark
   b) **36** 1 mark   d) **60** 1 mark
2. a) **9** 1 mark   c) **6** 1 mark
   b) **8** 1 mark   d) **12** 1 mark
3. a) **3** 1 mark   c) **54** 1 mark
   b) **7** 1 mark   d) **12** 1 mark
4. a) **36** 1 mark   b) **8** 1 mark
5. 4 × 5 = **20 minutes** 1 mark
6. 10 × 12 = **120 stickers** 1 mark
7. 3 + 4 = 7. 6 × 7 = **42 beads**
   2 marks for the correct answer,
   otherwise 1 mark for the correct working.
8. 4 + 6 = 10. 10 × 5 = **50 pieces**
   2 marks for the correct answer,
   otherwise 1 mark for the correct working.

Puzzle: Time for Doughnuts

10 × 6 = 60
2 × 5 = 10
60 + 10 = 70

12 × 6 = 72

2 × 12 = 24
10 × 5 = 50
24 + 50 = 74

8 × 12 = 96

Workout 2 — pages 4-5

1. a) **21** 1 mark   c) **49** 1 mark
   b) **99** 1 mark   d) **110** 1 mark
2. a) **2** 1 mark   c) **11** 1 mark
   b) **6** 1 mark   d) **11** 1 mark
3. a) **4** 1 mark   c) **2** 1 mark
   b) **7** 1 mark   d) **11** 1 mark
4. a) **8** 1 mark   b) **88** 1 mark
5. 7 × 5 = **35 tulips** 1 mark
6. 3 × 11 = **33 facts** 1 mark
7. 7 × 4 = 28. 100 − 28 = **72 sequins**
   2 marks for the correct answer,
   otherwise 1 mark for the correct working.
8. 5 + 7 = 12. 12 × 7 = **84 decorations**
   2 marks for the correct answer,
   otherwise 1 mark for the correct working.

Puzzle: Video Game Time

Kia (55 ÷ 5 = 11 minutes).
7 × 10 = 70. 11 × 6 = 66.
70 − 66 = **4 minutes**.
132 ÷ 11 = 12. 12 × 7 = **84 minutes**

Workout 3 — pages 6-7

1. a) **18** 1 mark   c) **63** 1 mark
   b) **81** 1 mark   d) **108** 1 mark
2. a) **6** 1 mark   c) **9** 1 mark
   b) **7** 1 mark   d) **5** 1 mark
3. a) **72** 1 mark   c) **10** 1 mark
   b) **1** 1 mark   d) **5** 1 mark
4. a) **27** 1 mark   b) **27** 1 mark
5.
   ```
       2 6              1 0 7
   ×     9          ×       9
   -------          ---------
     2 3 4            9 6 3
       5    1 mark        6    1 mark
   ```
6. 81 ÷ 9 = **9 party bags** 1 mark
7. 36 ÷ 9 = **4 minutes** 1 mark
8. 10 × 9 = 90. 145 − 90 = **55 kg**
   2 marks for the correct answer,
   otherwise 1 mark for the correct working.

Puzzle: Poorly Piggy

The number is bigger than 2 × 9 = 18,
but smaller than 9 × 11 = 99. So it can't be 108.
It's bigger than 9 × 5 = 45. So it can't be 27.
54 ÷ 9 = 6. 72 ÷ 9 = 8.
8 is bigger than 7 so the number of the poorly pig is **72**

Workout 4 — pages 8-9

1. a) **6** 1 mark   c) **44** 1 mark
   b) **72** 1 mark   d) **72** 1 mark
2. a) **10** 1 mark   c) **12** 1 mark
   b) **3** 1 mark   d) **9** 1 mark
3. a) **64** 1 mark   c) **7** 1 mark
   b) **2** 1 mark   d) **7** 1 mark
4. a) **12** 1 mark   b) **84** 1 mark
5. 11 × 3 = **33 g** 1 mark
6. 4 × 3 = **12 bags** 1 mark
7. £8.00 × 6 = £48.00.
   £48.00 + £4.50 = **£52.50**
   2 marks for the correct answer,
   otherwise 1 mark for the correct working.
8. 1 hour 20 minutes = 60 + 20 = 80 minutes.
   80 ÷ 8 = **10 minutes**
   2 marks for the correct answer,
   otherwise 1 mark for the correct working.

Puzzle: Fun at the Fair

3 × £3 = £9. 3 × £2 = £6. £9 + £6 = **£15**
6 × £3 = £18. £20 − £18 = **£2**
3 × £5 = £15. 5 × £8 = £40. £15 + £40 = £55.
£55 − £50 = **£5**

Workout 5 — pages 10-11

1. a) **55** 1 mark   c) **44** 1 mark
   b) **5** 1 mark   d) **132** 1 mark
2. a) **3** 1 mark   c) **5** 1 mark
   b) **11** 1 mark   d) **1** 1 mark
3. a) **12** 1 mark   c) **11** 1 mark
   b) **11** 1 mark   d) **5** 1 mark
4. a) **20** 1 mark   b) **66** 1 mark
5. 110 ÷ 11 = **10 socks** 1 mark
6. 8 × 11 = 88. 100 − 88 = **12 bunches**
   2 marks for the correct answer,
   otherwise 1 mark for the correct working.
7. 11 × 4 = 44. 5 × 2 = 10.
   44 + 10 = **54 drawing pins**
   3 marks for the correct answer, otherwise
   1 mark for each correct multiplication.

Puzzle: Bath Time

Workout 6 — pages 12-13

1. a) **66** 1 mark   c) **18** 1 mark
   b) **12** 1 mark   d) **28** 1 mark
2. a) **6** 1 mark   c) **11** 1 mark
   b) **5** 1 mark   d) **12** 1 mark
3. a) **99** 1 mark   c) **7** 1 mark
   b) **8** 1 mark   d) **60** 1 mark
4. a) **11** 1 mark   b) **49** 1 mark
5. a) 6 × 7 = **42 birds** 1 mark
   b) 18 ÷ 6 = **3 days** 1 mark
6. 21 ÷ 3 = **7 litres** 1 mark
7. 3 × 7 = 21. 4 × 6 = 24.
   21 + 24 = **45 hours**
   3 marks for the correct answer, otherwise
   1 mark for each correct multiplication.

Puzzle: Clowning Around

6 × 2 = **12 people**

3 clowns should be drawn on the pictogram for the evening.

36 ÷ 6 = **6 days**

Workout 7 — pages 14-15

1. a) **45** 1 mark   c) **32** 1 mark
   b) **4** 1 mark   d) **27** 1 mark
2. a) **1** 1 mark   c) **10** 1 mark
   b) **9** 1 mark   d) **9** 1 mark
3. a) **5** 1 mark   c) **99** 1 mark
   b) **11** 1 mark   d) **2** 1 mark
4. a) **12** 1 mark   b) **24** 1 mark
5. 9 × 2 = **18 tyres** 1 mark
6. 36 ÷ 4 = **9 teaspoons** 1 mark
7. 36 ÷ 4 = 9. 10 − 9 = **1 page**
   2 marks for the correct answer,
   otherwise 1 mark for the correct working.
8. $9\overline{)3\,{}^37\,{}^18}$ = **42** 1 mark $4\overline{)1\,{}^18\,{}^24}$ = **46** 1 mark

Puzzle: Fluttering Around

Butterfly A: Moves 5 squares south = (**2**, **4**)
Butterfly B: Moves 8 squares south
and 4 squares east = (**12**, **0**)
Butterfly C: Moves 9 squares north and
9 squares west = (**1**, **10**)

Workout 8 — pages 16-17

1. a) **90** 1 mark   c) **48** 1 mark
   b) **24** 1 mark   d) **108** 1 mark
2. a) **9** 1 mark   c) **12** 1 mark
   b) **5** 1 mark   d) **1** 1 mark
3. a) **9** 1 mark   c) **3** 1 mark
   b) **9** 1 mark   d) **4** 1 mark
4. a) **64** 1 mark   b) **88** 1 mark
5. 2 × 8 = **16 strawberries** 1 mark
6. 6 × 9 = **54 lockers** 1 mark
7. £4 × 9 = £36. £36 − £12 = **£24**
   2 marks for the correct answer,
   otherwise 1 mark for the correct working.
8. 9 × 9 = 81 jumps. **80 jumps** to the nearest 10.
   2 marks for the correct answer,
   otherwise 1 mark for the correct working.

Puzzle: Cleaning Bonus!

Rosie cleaned $\frac{1}{8}$ of 8 windows. 8 ÷ 8 = **1 window**.
Garret cleaned $\frac{1}{8}$ of 16 windows. 16 ÷ 8 = **2 windows**.

Nelly cleaned $\frac{2}{9}$ of 18 windows.
18 ÷ 9 = 2. 2 × 2 = 4 windows.
Quentin cleaned $\frac{3}{8}$ of 16 windows.
16 ÷ 8 = 2. 2 × 3 = 6 windows.
So **Nelly** and **Quentin** will get a bonus.

Workout 9 — pages 18-19

1. a) **120** 1 mark   c) **24** 1 mark
   b) **54** 1 mark   d) **42** 1 mark
2. a) **12** 1 mark   c) **2** 1 mark
   b) **5** 1 mark   d) **12** 1 mark
3. a) **12** 1 mark   c) **9** 1 mark
   b) **11** 1 mark   d) **8** 1 mark
4. a) **1** 1 mark   b) **22** 1 mark
5. 　　2 3 4　　　　　　9 4 6
   ×　　　2　　　　×　　　6
   ─────────　　　─────────
   　　4 6 8　　　　5 6 7 6
   　　　　　1 mark　　 ₂ ₃ 　 1 mark
6. 8 × 9 = 72. 100 − 72 = **28 candles**
   2 marks for the correct answer,
   otherwise 1 mark for the correct working.
7. 50 − 2 = 48. 48 ÷ 4 = **12 children**
   2 marks for the correct answer,
   otherwise 1 mark for the correct working.

Puzzle: Locked Boxes
Key A opens box **H**. It contains **60** jewels.
Key B opens box **E**. It contains **30** jewels.
Key C opens box **G**. It contains **54** jewels.
Key D opens box **F**. It contains **81** jewels.

Workout 10 — pages 20-21

1. a) **22** 1 mark   c) **11** 1 mark
   b) **55** 1 mark   d) **44** 1 mark
2. a) **7** 1 mark   c) **8** 1 mark
   b) **9** 1 mark   d) **11** 1 mark
3. a) **11** 1 mark   c) **66** 1 mark
   b) **11** 1 mark   d) **1** 1 mark
4. a) **110** 1 mark   b) **11** 1 mark
5. 4 × 11 × 2 = 8 × 11 = **88 kilometres**
   2 marks for the correct answer,
   otherwise 1 mark for the correct working.
6. 200 − 68 = 132. 132 ÷ 11 = **12 bird boxes**
   2 marks for the correct answer,
   otherwise 1 mark for the correct working.
7. £2 + £2 + £5 = £9. £9 × 11 = **£99**
   2 marks for the correct answer,
   otherwise 1 mark for the correct working.

Puzzle: Harri's Hamsters
11 × 5 = **55 scoops of sawdust**
11 × 2 = 22. 22 − 15 = **7 food bowls**
11 × 3 = 33 tubes. So Harri will need to buy
4 packs (4 × 10 = 40 tubes).

Workout 11 — pages 22-23

1. a) **108** 1 mark   c) **80** 1 mark
   b) **50** 1 mark   d) **84** 1 mark
2. a) **9** 1 mark   c) **10** 1 mark
   b) **3** 1 mark   d) **12** 1 mark
3. a) **10** 1 mark   c) **6** 1 mark
   b) **10** 1 mark   d) **12** 1 mark
4. a) **18** 1 mark   b) **6** 1 mark
5. 6 × 12 = **72 questions** 1 mark
6. £48 ÷ 4 = £12. £12 − £4.75 = **£7.25**
   2 marks for the correct answer,
   otherwise 1 mark for the correct working.
7. a) 9 × 7 = **63 hearts** 1 mark
   b) 84 ÷ 7 = **12 cm** 1 mark
   c) 12 ÷ 3 = **4 cm** 1 mark

Puzzle: Wendy's Potions

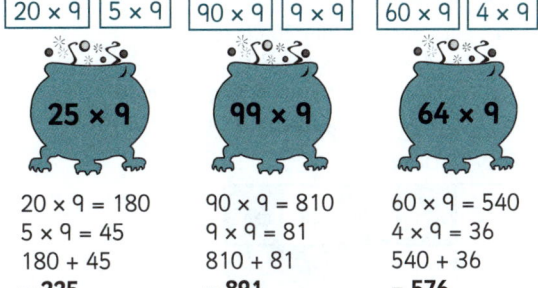

20 × 9 = 180　　90 × 9 = 810　　60 × 9 = 540
5 × 9 = 45　　　9 × 9 = 81　　　4 × 9 = 36
180 + 45　　　　810 + 81　　　　540 + 36
= **225**　　　　= **891**　　　　= **576**

Workout 12 — pages 24-25

1. a) **44** 1 mark   c) **18** 1 mark
   b) **56** 1 mark   d) **72** 1 mark
2. a) **8** 1 mark   c) **12** 1 mark
   b) **7** 1 mark   d) **3** 1 mark
3. a) **9** 1 mark   c) **11** 1 mark
   b) **6** 1 mark   d) **9** 1 mark
4. a) **64** 1 mark   b) **70** 1 mark
5. 7 × 7 = 49. 49 − 12 = **37 steps**
   2 marks for the correct answer,
   otherwise 1 mark for the correct working.
6. 9 × 7 = 63. 63 − 30 = **33 tins**
   2 marks for the correct answer,
   otherwise 1 mark for the correct working.

7.
    5 6
    7⟌3 ³9 ⁴2   1 mark

    1 6
    8⟌1 ¹2 ⁴8   1 mark

Puzzle: Rachael's New Clothes!

3 × 7 = **21 outfits**

4 × 3 × 7 = 12 × 7 = **84 outfits**

84 ÷ 7 = **12 weeks**

Spring Term

Workout 1 — pages 26-27

1. a) **12** 1 mark   c) **84** 1 mark
   b) **35** 1 mark   d) **54** 1 mark
2. a) **3** 1 mark   c) **8** 1 mark
   b) **7** 1 mark   d) **6** 1 mark
3. a) **3** 1 mark   c) **7** 1 mark
   b) **9** 1 mark   d) **4** 1 mark
4. a) **48** 1 mark   b) **2** 1 mark
5. a) 3 × 7 = **£21** 1 mark
   b) 6 × 2 = £12. £12 + £3 = **£15**
      2 marks for the correct answer,
      otherwise 1 mark for the correct working.
6. 6 × 11 = **66 apples** 1 mark
7. a) Lucy needs to buy 26 apples.
      6 × 4 = 24. 6 × 5 = 30.
      So Lucy needs to buy **5 bags**. 1 mark
   b) 30 − 26 = **4 apples** 1 mark

Puzzle: Disco Dilemma

12	89	44	24	51
35	72	77	19	55
46	75	16	21	64
54	30	52	63	18
81	40	22	7	39

Workout 2 — pages 28-29

1. a) **45** 1 mark   c) **72** 1 mark
   b) **110** 1 mark   d) **28** 1 mark
2. a) **4** 1 mark   c) **8** 1 mark
   b) **6** 1 mark   d) **9** 1 mark
3. a) **7** 1 mark   c) **2** 1 mark
   b) **12** 1 mark   d) **3** 1 mark
4. a) **80** 1 mark   b) **84** 1 mark
5. 3 × 12 = **36 jam tarts** 1 mark
6. 35 ÷ 7 = **5 weeks** 1 mark

7. 14 ÷ 2 = 7. 3 × 7 = **21 years old**
   2 marks for the correct answer,
   otherwise 1 mark for the correct working.
8. a) 8 × 10 = **80 black pens** 1 mark
   b) 24 ÷ 3 = **8 packs** 1 mark

Puzzle: How Old?

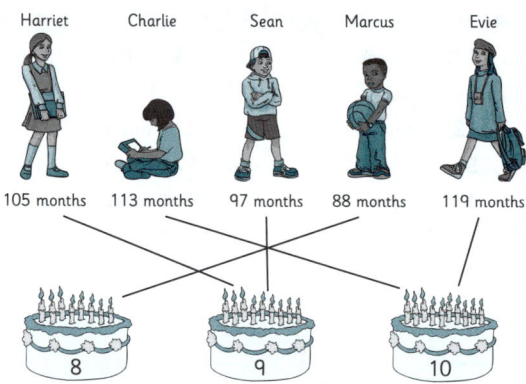

Workout 3 — pages 30-31

1. a) **108** 1 mark   c) **66** 1 mark
   b) **44** 1 mark   d) **18** 1 mark
2. a) **8** 1 mark   c) **2** 1 mark
   b) **8** 1 mark   d) **6** 1 mark
3. a) **11** 1 mark   c) **10** 1 mark
   b) **11** 1 mark   d) **9** 1 mark
4. a) **121** 1 mark   b) **10** 1 mark
5. 8 × 11 = **88 certificates** 1 mark
6. 63 ÷ 7 = 9. 9 × 2 = **18 alpacas**
   2 marks for the correct answer,
   otherwise 1 mark for the correct working.
7. 9 × 4 = 36. 11 × 2 = 22.
   36 − 22 = **14 miles**
   3 marks for the correct answer, otherwise
   1 mark for each correct multiplication.

Puzzle: A Game of Cards

Workout 4 — pages 32-33

1. a) **77** 1 mark c) **40** 1 mark
   b) **45** 1 mark d) **96** 1 mark
2. a) **5** 1 mark   c) **3** 1 mark
   b) **10** 1 mark d) **6** 1 mark
3. a) **4** 1 mark   c) **12** 1 mark
   b) **5** 1 mark   d) **12** 1 mark
4. a) **70** 1 mark b) **4** 1 mark
5. $84 \div 12 = 7$. $2 \times 7 =$ **14 eggs**
   2 marks for the correct answer,
   otherwise 1 mark for the correct working.
6. $3 \times 7 = 21$. $36 - 21 =$ **£15**
   2 marks for the correct answer,
   otherwise 1 mark for the correct working.
7. $58 - 3 = 55$. $55 \div 5 =$ **11 biscuits**
   2 marks for the correct answer,
   otherwise 1 mark for the correct working.

Puzzle: Ancient Amounts
VII × IV = XXVIII
$7 \times 4 = 28$
VI × XII = LXXII
$6 \times 12 = 72$
V × VII = XXXV
$5 \times 7 = 35$
II × X = XX
$2 \times 10 = 20$

Workout 5 — pages 34-35

1. a) **10** 1 mark   c) **132** 1 mark
   b) **70** 1 mark   d) **18** 1 mark
2. a) **12** 1 mark   c) **1** 1 mark
   b) **10** 1 mark   d) **5** 1 mark
3. a) **11** 1 mark   c) **6** 1 mark
   b) **4** 1 mark   d) **8** 1 mark
4. a) **8** 1 mark   b) **4** 1 mark
5.
   ```
       7 2            3 0 6
     ×   7          ×     2
     -----          -------
     5 0 4          6 1 2
       1              1
   ```
   1 mark   1 mark
6. $7 \times 7 =$ **49 days** 1 mark
7. $12\ m \times 12\ m = 144\ m^2$. $7 \times 3 = 21\ m^2$.
   $144\ m^2 + 21\ m^2 =$ **165 m²**
   3 marks for the correct answer, otherwise
   1 mark for each correct multiplication.

Puzzle: At the Garden Centre
$42 \div 7 = 6$, so $420 \div 7 =$ **60 trays of marigolds**
$48 \div 12 = 4$, so $480 \div 12 =$ **40 trays of pansies**
$24 \div 2 = 12$, so $240 \div 2 =$ **120 trays of geraniums**

Workout 6 — pages 36-37

1. a) **11** 1 mark   c) **25** 1 mark
   b) **36** 1 mark   d) **72** 1 mark
2. a) **9** 1 mark   c) **5** 1 mark
   b) **12** 1 mark   d) **11** 1 mark
3. a) **2** 1 mark   c) **3** 1 mark
   b) **6** 1 mark   d) **11** 1 mark
4. a) **60** 1 mark   b) **88** 1 mark
5. $6 \times 7 =$ **42 eggs** 1 mark
6. $12 \times 2 = 24$. $6 \times 3 = 18$.
   $24 + 18 =$ **42 people**
   3 marks for the correct answer, otherwise
   1 mark for each correct multiplication.
7.
   ```
         1 6 7                9 4
     5 ) 8³3³5    1 mark   6 ) 5⁵6²4    1 mark
   ```

Puzzle: At the Sweet Shop
$8 \times 6p = 48p$. $9 \times 5p = 45p$. $2 \times 11p = 22p$.
$48p + 45p + 22p = 115p$.
£3 = 300p
$300p - 115p = 185p =$ **£1.85**
$30 \div 6 = 5$, so $300p \div 6 =$ **50 foam mushrooms**

Workout 7 — pages 38-39

1. a) **24** 1 mark   c) **84** 1 mark
   b) **60** 1 mark   d) **36** 1 mark
2. a) **4** 1 mark   c) **3** 1 mark
   b) **11** 1 mark   d) **5** 1 mark
3. a) **1** 1 mark   c) **8** 1 mark
   b) **7** 1 mark   d) **9** 1 mark
4. a) **96** 1 mark   b) **108** 1 mark
5. $12 \times 4 = 48$. $48 - 35 =$ **13 people**
   2 marks for the correct answer,
   otherwise 1 mark for the correct working.
6. $2 \times 12 = 24$ white sweets.
   $12 + 24 =$ **36 sweets**.
   2 marks for the correct answer,
   otherwise 1 mark for the correct working.
7. $6 \times 12 = 72$. $72 - 64 =$ **8 eggs**
   2 marks for the correct answer,
   otherwise 1 mark for the correct working.

Puzzle: Pie Proportions
$12 \div 12 = 1$. $48 \div 12 = 4$. So $\frac{12}{48} = \frac{1}{4}$
$60 \div 12 = 5$. $72 \div 12 = 6$. So $\frac{60}{72} = \frac{5}{6}$
$12 \div 12 = 1$. $24 \div 12 = 2$. So $\frac{12}{24} = \frac{1}{2}$
$24 \div 12 = 2$. $36 \div 12 = 3$. So $\frac{24}{36} = \frac{2}{3}$

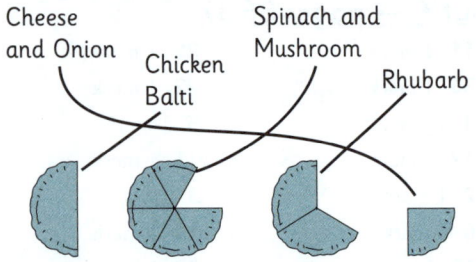

The largest amount sold is of **spinach and mushroom**.

Workout 8 — pages 40-41

1. a) **12** 1 mark   c) **27** 1 mark
   b) **35** 1 mark   d) **42** 1 mark
2. a) **7** 1 mark   c) **7** 1 mark
   b) **2** 1 mark   d) **10** 1 mark
3. a) **3** 1 mark   c) **8** 1 mark
   b) **6** 1 mark   d) **9** 1 mark
4. a) **6** 1 mark   b) **11** 1 mark
5. 4 × 7 = 28. 28 − 3 = **25 cupcakes**
   2 marks for the correct answer,
   otherwise 1 mark for the correct working.
6. 3 × 6 = 18, so 3 × 60 = 180.
   180 + 40 = **220 minutes**
   2 marks for the correct answer,
   otherwise 1 mark for the correct working.
7. 12 cm + 72 cm = 84 cm.
   84 ÷ 12 = **7 times longer**
   2 marks for the correct answer,
   otherwise 1 mark for the correct working.

Puzzle: Football Figures

a)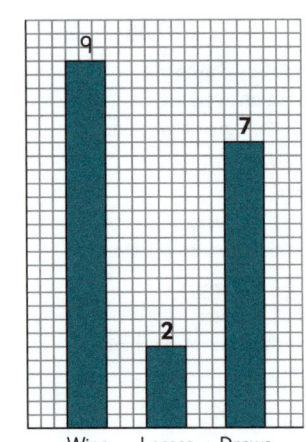

b) 3 × 9 = 27. 1 × 7 = 7. 0 × 2 = 0.
   27 + 7 + 0 = **34 points**

Workout 9 — pages 42-43

1. a) **16** 1 mark   c) **9** 1 mark
   b) **55** 1 mark   d) **20** 1 mark

2. a) **12** 1 mark   c) **12** 1 mark
   b) **8** 1 mark   d) **8** 1 mark
3. a) **9** 1 mark   c) **7** 1 mark
   b) **7** 1 mark   d) **6** 1 mark
4. a) **32** 1 mark   b) **9** 1 mark
5.
   ```
     3 3            2 4 0
   ×   7          ×     4
   ─────          ───────
   2 3 1          9 6 0
     2              1
   ```
   1 mark   1 mark
6. 4 × 3 = **12 T-shirts** 1 mark
7. a) 11 × 3 = 33. 11 × 4 = 44.
      So they can send **3 teams**.
      2 marks for the correct answer,
      otherwise 1 mark for the correct working.
   b) 44 − 39 = **5 more members** 1 mark

Puzzle: Pizza Possibilities

4 × 6 = **24 pizzas**

5 + 1 = 6. 6 × 4 = 24. 24 ÷ 8 = 3. So the smallest number of pizzas Katja can buy is **3 pizzas**.

Workout 10 — pages 44-45

1. a) **56** 1 mark   c) **15** 1 mark
   b) **66** 1 mark   d) **45** 1 mark
2. a) **8** 1 mark   c) **12** 1 mark
   b) **3** 1 mark   d) **7** 1 mark
3. a) **6** 1 mark   c) **4** 1 mark
   b) **2** 1 mark   d) **5** 1 mark
4. a) **16** 1 mark   b) **2** 1 mark
5. a) 9 × 3 = 27. 3 × 8 = 24. 4 × 8 = 32.
      So she needs to buy **4 packets of stickers**.
      2 marks for the correct answer,
      otherwise 1 mark for the correct working.
   b) 32 − 27 = **5 stickers** 1 mark
6. 11p × 5 = 55p. 8p × 6 = 48p.
   55p − 48p = **7p**
   3 marks for the correct answer,
   otherwise 1 mark for each correct multiplication.

Puzzle: Humphrey's Hats

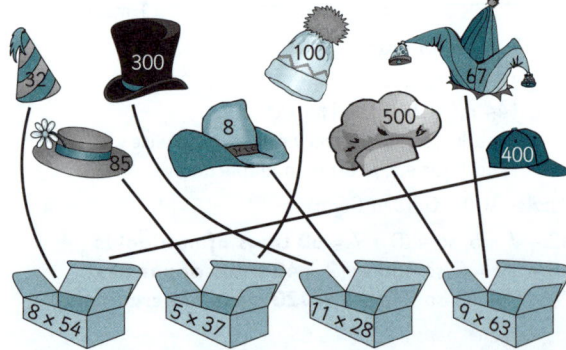

Workout 11 — pages 46-47
1. a) **30** 1 mark   c) **81** 1 mark
   b) **72** 1 mark   d) **36** 1 mark
2. a) **10** 1 mark   c) **1** 1 mark
   b) **11** 1 mark   d) **5** 1 mark
3. a) **7** 1 mark   c) **12** 1 mark
   b) **3** 1 mark   d) **12** 1 mark
4. a) **108** 1 mark   b) **72** 1 mark
5. 6 × 4 = 24. 24 − 7 = **17 pieces**
   2 marks for the correct answer,
   otherwise 1 mark for the correct working.
6. 2 × 9 = 18, so 20 × 9 = **180 ml**
   2 marks for the correct answer,
   otherwise 1 mark for the correct working.
7. 36 ÷ 9 = 4.
   4 × 6 = **24 minutes**
   2 marks for the correct answer,
   otherwise 1 mark for the correct working.

Puzzle: Finley's Special Punch

Special punch for **54** people

27 cups lemonade

18 cups tomato juice

45 teaspoons maple syrup

36 teaspoons cinnamon

63 drops peppermint extract

108 glacé cherries

Workout 12 — pages 48-49
1. a) **8** 1 mark   c) **44** 1 mark
   b) **54** 1 mark   d) **20** 1 mark
2. a) **7** 1 mark   c) **11** 1 mark
   b) **3** 1 mark   d) **9** 1 mark
3. a) **1** 1 mark   c) **8** 1 mark
   b) **6** 1 mark   d) **9** 1 mark
4. a) **55** 1 mark   b) **8** 1 mark
5. 4 × 2 = 8 classes. 8 × 9 = **72 pupils**
   2 marks for the correct answer,
   otherwise 1 mark for the correct working.
6. 33 ÷ 11 = 3. 3 × 9 = **27 trees**
   2 marks for the correct answer,
   otherwise 1 mark for the correct working.
7. 2) 7^{1}5^{1}2 = 376   1 mark
   9) 2^{2}4^{6}3 = 27   1 mark

Puzzle: Present Problems

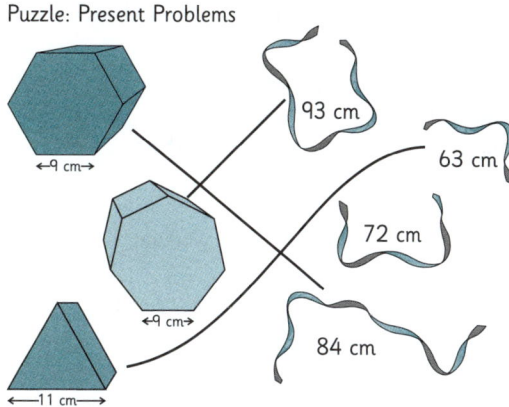

Summer Term
Workout 1 — pages 50-51
1. a) **16** 1 mark   c) **88** 1 mark
   b) **36** 1 mark   d) **48** 1 mark
2. a) **12** 1 mark   c) **7** 1 mark
   b) **5** 1 mark   d) **10** 1 mark
3. a) **8** 1 mark   c) **120** 1 mark
   b) **11** 1 mark   d) **12** 1 mark
4. a) **6** 1 mark   b) **108** 1 mark
5. £12 × 7 = **£84**   1 mark
6. 8 × 6 = **48 seeds**   1 mark
7. 3 + 5 = 8. 8 × 4 = **32 seconds**
   2 marks for the correct answer,
   otherwise 1 mark for the correct working.
8. 250 − 210 = 40. 40 ÷ 8 = **5 children**
   2 marks for the correct answer,
   otherwise 1 mark for the correct working.

Puzzle: New Boat!
Year 4 trip from local school:
Old boat = 24 ÷ 8 = **3 journeys**
New boat = 24 ÷ 12 = **2 journeys**
Coachload of tourists:
Old boat = 72 ÷ 8 = **9 journeys**
New boat = 72 ÷ 12 = **6 journeys**
Open-air concert audience:
Old boat = 96 ÷ 8 = **12 journeys**
New boat = 96 ÷ 12 = **8 journeys**

Workout 2 — pages 52-53
1. a) **12** 1 mark   c) **72** 1 mark
   b) **55** 1 mark   d) **56** 1 mark
2. a) **7** 1 mark   c) **9** 1 mark
   b) **12** 1 mark   d) **7** 1 mark
3. a) **3** 1 mark   c) **70** 1 mark
   b) **132** 1 mark   d) **4** 1 mark
4. a) **48** 1 mark   b) **6** 1 mark

5. 7 × 9 = **63 grams** 1 mark
6. 99p ÷ 11 = **9p** 1 mark
7. 4 × 7 = 28. 50 − 28 = **22 ml**
   2 marks for the correct answer,
   otherwise 1 mark for the correct working.
8. 6 × 3 = 18. 18 + 3 = **21 bandages**
   2 marks for the correct answer,
   otherwise 1 mark for the correct working.

Puzzle: Under the Sea

Weight of the Merking's Magic Rock = 4 × 9 = 36 g
11 × 3 = 33 g, 8 × 4 = 32 g, 5 × 7 = 35 g,
7 × 6 = 42 g, so the **5 × 7** shell should be circled.

Workout 3 — pages 54-55

1. a) **36** 1 mark   c) **20** 1 mark
   b) **77** 1 mark   d) **21** 1 mark
2. a) **12** 1 mark   c) **11** 1 mark
   b) **12** 1 mark   d) **7** 1 mark
3. a) **6** 1 mark   c) **5** 1 mark
   b) **4** 1 mark   d) **6** 1 mark
4. a) **60** 1 mark   b) **110** 1 mark
5. 9 × 10 = **90 tiles** 1 mark
6. 3 × 3 = **9 m** 1 mark
7. 4 × 7 = 28. 28 × 10 = **280 pieces of fruit**
   2 marks for the correct answer,
   otherwise 1 mark for the correct working.
8. 27 ÷ 3 = 9. 27 − 9 = **18 children**
   2 marks for the correct answer,
   otherwise 1 mark for the correct working.

Puzzle: Sale Time!

Microphone: £12 ÷ 3 = £4. £12 − £4 = **£8**
Clock radio: £35 ÷ 7 = £5. £35 − 5 = **£30**
Headphones: £60 ÷ 10 = £6. £6 × 3 = £18.
  £60 − £18 = **£42**
Phone: £21 ÷ 3 = £7. £7 × 2 = £14.
  £21 − 14 = **£7**

Workout 4 — pages 56-57

1. a) **60** 1 mark   c) **28** 1 mark
   b) **18** 1 mark   d) **21** 1 mark
2. a) **9** 1 mark   c) **10** 1 mark
   b) **11** 1 mark   d) **8** 1 mark
3. a) **6** 1 mark   c) **7** 1 mark
   b) **12** 1 mark   d) **4** 1 mark
4. a) **24** 1 mark   b) **84** 1 mark
5.
```
    4 8 5          1 9 8
  ×     4        ×     3
  ---------      ---------
  1 9 4 0          5 9 4
    3 2              2 2
```
1 mark   1 mark

6. 15 ÷ 3 = **5 songs** 1 mark
7. 4 × 3 = 12. 12 × 3 = 36.
   50 − 36 = **14 biscuits**
   3 marks for the correct answer, otherwise
   1 mark for each correct multiplication.

Puzzle: Mrs Vasso's Art Wall

Fox: Area = 9 × 4 = **36 in²**
Duck: Area = 12 × 12 = **144 in²**
Lobster: Area = 6 × 12 = **72 in²**
Shark: Area = 4 × 12 = **48 in²**
Hedgehog: Area = 3 × 4 = **12 in²**
3 m × 1 m = **3 m²**
3 × 12 = **36 inches**

Workout 5 — pages 58-59

1. a) **22** 1 mark   c) **54** 1 mark
   b) **84** 1 mark   d) **18** 1 mark
2. a) **12** 1 mark   c) **8** 1 mark
   b) **4** 1 mark   d) **11** 1 mark
3. a) **4** 1 mark   c) **42** 1 mark
   b) **88** 1 mark   d) **9** 1 mark
4. a) **110** 1 mark   b) **63** 1 mark
5. 8p × 7 = **56p** 1 mark
6. 1 m = 100 cm
   9 × 11 cm = 99 cm. 10 × 11 cm = 110 cm.
   So Skylar needs to use **10 bricks**.
   2 marks for the correct answer,
   otherwise 1 mark for the correct working.
7. 5 × £6 = £30. £70 − £30 = £40.
   £40 ÷ 5 = **£8**
   3 marks for the correct answer, otherwise
   1 mark for subtracting the cinema cost from
   the total and 1 mark for dividing by 5.

Puzzle: Connie's Coconuts

Connie could get **2** or **3** coconuts.

Workout 6 — pages 60-61

1. a) **35** 1 mark   c) **63** 1 mark
   b) **7** 1 mark   d) **28** 1 mark
2. a) **11** 1 mark   c) **12** 1 mark
   b) **7** 1 mark   d) **8** 1 mark

3. a) **10** 1 mark   c) **7** 1 mark
    b) **14** 1 mark   d) **6** 1 mark
4. a) **10** 1 mark   b) **77** 1 mark
5.   **4 0 7**   **8 3 r3**
    7) 2 ²8 4 ⁴9 1 mark   7) 5 ⁵8 ²4 1 mark
6. 12 × 7 = **84 people** 1 mark
7. 6 × 7 = 42. 9 × 7 = 63.
    42 + 63 = **105 millilitres**
    3 marks for the correct answer, otherwise
    1 mark for each correct multiplication.

Puzzle: Story Book Characters
7 × 2 = **14 pounds**
14 ÷ 2 = 7. 5 × 7 = **35 centimetres**
7 × 3 = **21 feet** and 15 ÷ 5 × 2 = 3 × 2 = **6 inches**

Workout 7 — pages 62-63

1. a) **24** 1 mark   c) **63** 1 mark
    b) **33** 1 mark   d) **48** 1 mark
2. a) **9** 1 mark   c) **2** 1 mark
    b) **5** 1 mark   d) **6** 1 mark
3. a) **2** 1 mark   c) **11** 1 mark
    b) **7** 1 mark   d) **4** 1 mark
4. a) **56** 1 mark   b) **81** 1 mark
5. 4 × 2 = 8. 88 ÷ 8 = **11 days**
    2 marks for the correct answer,
    otherwise 1 mark for the correct working.
6. 5 × 7 = 35. 60 − 35 = **25 pages**
    2 marks for the correct answer,
    otherwise 1 mark for the correct working.
7. 4 × 100 = 400.
    4 × 9 = 36. So 400 × 9 = **3600 m**
    2 marks for the correct answer,
    otherwise 1 mark for the correct working.

Puzzle: Hattie's Tea Party

Workout 8 — pages 64-65

1. a) **54** 1 mark   c) **24** 1 mark
    b) **84** 1 mark   d) **132** 1 mark
2. a) **2** 1 mark   c) **9** 1 mark
    b) **2** 1 mark   d) **4** 1 mark
3. a) **5** 1 mark   c) **9** 1 mark
    b) **3** 1 mark   d) **3** 1 mark
4. a) **108** 1 mark   b) **6** 1 mark
5. 8 × 12 = **96 months** 1 mark
6. 5 × 8 = 40. 7 × 9 = 63.
    40 + 63 = **103 spots**
    3 marks for the correct answer, otherwise
    1 mark for each correct multiplication.
7.

                                            7 5
                                         × 1 2
            1 2 1 4   1 5 0
     ×   6   + 7 5 0
     7 2 8 4   **9 0 0**
      1 2   1 mark   1   1 mark

Puzzle: Ted's in Trouble

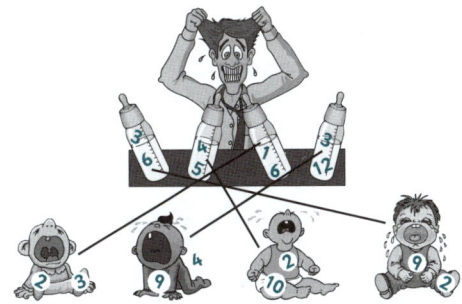

Workout 9 — pages 66-67

1. a) **72** 1 mark   c) **42** 1 mark
    b) **48** 1 mark   d) **54** 1 mark
2. a) **12** 1 mark   c) **1** 1 mark
    b) **11** 1 mark   d) **2** 1 mark
3. a) **4** 1 mark   c) **10** 1 mark
    b) **6** 1 mark   d) **5** 1 mark
4. a) **24** 1 mark   b) **3** 1 mark
5. 48 ÷ 6 = **8 radishes** 1 mark
6. 15 ÷ 5 = 3. 3 × 6 = **18 cheese sandwiches**
    2 marks for the correct answer,
    otherwise 1 mark for the correct working.
7. 6 × 2 = 12. So 6 × 20 = 120 cm.
    12 × 4 = 48. So 120 × 4 = **480 cm**
    3 marks for the correct answer,
    otherwise 1 mark for multiplying by 20
    and 1 mark for multiplying by 4.

Puzzle: How Far?

Library $2\frac{5}{6}$ miles

Museum $4\frac{1}{6}$ miles

Beach $1\frac{4}{6}$ miles (or $1\frac{2}{3}$ miles)

Park $6\frac{3}{6}$ miles (or $6\frac{1}{2}$ miles)

Workout 10 — pages 68-69

1. a) **50** 1 mark   c) **88** 1 mark
   b) **84** 1 mark   d) **20** 1 mark
2. a) **8** 1 mark   c) **12** 1 mark
   b) **2** 1 mark   d) **4** 1 mark
3. a) **2** 1 mark   c) **4** 1 mark
   b) **4** 1 mark   d) **12** 1 mark
4. a) **60** 1 mark   b) **100** 1 mark
5. 42 ÷ 7 = **6 tubs of paint** 1 mark
6. 4 × 10 = 40. 40 + 6 = **46 plates**
   2 marks for the correct answer,
   otherwise 1 mark for the correct working.
7. 8 × 7 = 56. 9 × 7 = 63.
   56 + 63 = **119 star jumps**
   3 marks for the correct answer,
   otherwise 1 mark for each correct multiplication.

Puzzle: Which Keys?

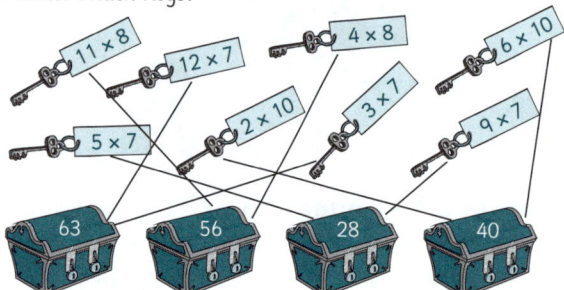

Workout 11 — pages 70-71

1. a) **21** 1 mark   c) **88** 1 mark
   b) **50** 1 mark   d) **49** 1 mark
2. a) **10** 1 mark   c) **1** 1 mark
   b) **3** 1 mark   d) **5** 1 mark
3. a) **12** 1 mark   c) **6** 1 mark
   b) **9** 1 mark   d) **8** 1 mark
4. a) **90** 1 mark   b) **5** 1 mark
5.   **3 9 1**
   7) 2²7⁶3 7   1 mark

         5 4 r 3
   9) 4⁴8³9   1 mark

6. 6 ÷ 2 = 3. 3 × 12 = **36 hair bands**
   2 marks for the correct answer,
   otherwise 1 mark for the correct working.
7. 72 ÷ 12 = 6. 6 × 9 = **54 seeds**
   2 marks for the correct answer,
   otherwise 1 mark for the correct working.

Puzzle: Add Up the Scores

Name	Questions Attempted	Correct Answers	Incorrect Answers	Points
Amir	12	5	7	**11**
Rosie	11	9	2	**41**
Inaya	**13**	8	5	30
Lily-Mae	12	**9**	3	**39**
Charles	13	7	**6**	**23**

Workout 12 — pages 72-73

1. a) **60** 1 mark   c) **28** 1 mark
   b) **36** 1 mark   d) **15** 1 mark
2. a) **1** 1 mark   c) **11** 1 mark
   b) **2** 1 mark   d) **2** 1 mark
3. a) **4** 1 mark   c) **7** 1 mark
   b) **3** 1 mark   d) **6** 1 mark
4. a) **132** 1 mark   b) **5** 1 mark
5. 9 × 5 = **45 hours** 1 mark
6. 27 ÷ 9 = 3. 15 ÷ 3 = **5 miles**
   2 marks for the correct answer,
   otherwise 1 mark for the correct working.
7. 4 × 5 = 20. 3 × 12 = 36. 20 + 36 = **£56**
   3 marks for the correct answer,
   otherwise 1 mark for each correct multiplication.

Puzzle: Say Cheese

$\frac{16}{36} = \frac{4}{9}$, $\frac{24}{72} = \frac{3}{9}$, $\frac{5}{45} = \frac{1}{9}$, $\frac{16}{18} = \frac{8}{9}$, $\frac{42}{54} = \frac{7}{9}$

Fay Mouse — **1**
Anonymouse — **2**
Squeaker — **3**
Enor Mouse — **4**
Julius Cheeser — **5**